W9-CMD-046

Worth Remembering

Irish-American Family Stories
of Seven Generations

And How to Write Your Family Tales

by
James J. Cuddy

Best Wishes!
James J. Cuddy
4/15/12

Worth Remembering
Irish-American Family Stories
of Seven Generations
And How to Write Your Family Tales

by

James J. Cuddy

First Edition
Copyright © 2004 by James J. Cuddy

Published by

Brundage Publishing
Room 203 Executive Office Building
33 West State Street
Binghamton, NY 13901

www.brundagepublishing.com

Jacket design by Amanda Nord

Library of Congress
Control Number: 2004106241

ISBN Number: 1-892451-22-0

Printed in the United States of America

Dedication

This book is dedicated to my wife and soul mate Joyce;

And to John and Veronica Cuddy, and Odilon and Irene LaCasse, our deceased parents;

And to youthful niece, Carolyn Cuddy, who died in 1980;

And to Joe and Ellie Lovely, friends and neighbors.

Acknowledgments

Special thanks go to my wife, Joyce, for her long-term support. She waited patiently, when I tied up the family computer on many occasions, and listened to the different drafts. Joyce intuitively understood my mission and goals, and made suggestions to help me stay on track.

I want to thank those who read drafts and advised with suggestions, and gave encouragement in many other ways: Barbara Blossom for three reviews; Margaret Hanson, Karen Elliott, and Marti Vasiliades for one review. Thanks go to Franklin Resseguie, wise and experienced publisher of Brundage Publishing, to Jennifer Sembler and Barrie Hoople for their steady and professional editing, and to Amanda Nord for her work on the jacket design. I'm also grateful for abiding general support, through the years, from John and Gloria Weyand, Mike and Heather O'Heaney, Joseph H. Phillips, Tom and Dotty Donnelly, Anne and Charlie Speicher, Chris Vasiliades, and the deceased Jeanne "Lady B" Bezek.

I mention Caroline, Carter, Cara, Jonah, Sarah, Julia, Noah, and Mia. These children renewed us whenever Joyce and I visited and played with them. Couples of the boomer generation gave inclusive hospitality: Johnny and Mary Yinger, Michael and Carol Grace, Barbara and I-Jian Lin.

Yes, and I almost forgot the Daughters of Charity who taught me to diagram sentences and encouraged my early attempts at writing over fifty-five years ago.

Table Of Contents

♣ Prologue ♣

♣ Family Tree ♣

♣ Chapter One ♣

♣ Chapter Two ♣

♣ Chapter Three ♣

♣ Chapter Four ♣

♣ Chapter Five ♣

♣ Chapter Six ♣

♣ Chapter Seven ♣

♣ Epilogue ♣

♣ Appendix ♣

Prologue

Our family, like most families, tells the same stories over and over. In this way we remember our roots. Frank McCourt regaled his English Literature students with darkly humorous accounts of his family life and urged them to write the family stories they heard or experienced. His students, in turn, pushed him to write a book about his family tales; he did so in *Angela's Ashes*.

A decade ago, I was designated our family's storyteller. At my brother Dave's wake, I primed the pump by telling some stories about him and our clan, and other relatives shared their tales. I later realized that our small family needed more than a designated storyteller; it needed a family story writer as well.

This is not a book of interest to Irish-American-Catholics alone. Readers with any immigrant history and from any ethnic, racial, or religious background may hear echoes of their experiences, from past generations to present, in my stories. Fully Americanized readers with only faint memories of their early ancestors may be prompted to wonder about their roots. I strove to write stories that would be universally engaging to a wide audience of readers, and motivational for some to gather, organize, and write their own family tales. I placed how-to hints about writing family stories in the Appendix.

This book includes family stories from seven generations, and I write from the fifth. I also playfully imagined and projected our family to the future eighth generation. The challenge of any family storyteller is to find the right voice: I discovered my reflective voice, which alternates between serious and lighthearted melodies. Like every family, we experienced the joys of birth and marriage and the pains of death and divorce, and when relating these events, each story required nuances of my basic voice.

I focused on many ancestors and current family members to balance my point of view. My approach was taken from the folklore of baseball umpires: "I called 'em like I saw 'em." A few times I used stories from non-family members because their tales have been grafted onto our family tree. I made this clear in the text.

Major events in the world today have changed our lives and history forever, but some things will not substantially change. We shall continue to tell family stories about different generations because they remind us of our identity and origins. They are the connecting threads of our personal and family history. Encouraged by these family constants, we can face the future, in whatever form, with measured confidence.

East Syracuse, NY
March 17, 2004

The Cuddy Family Tree

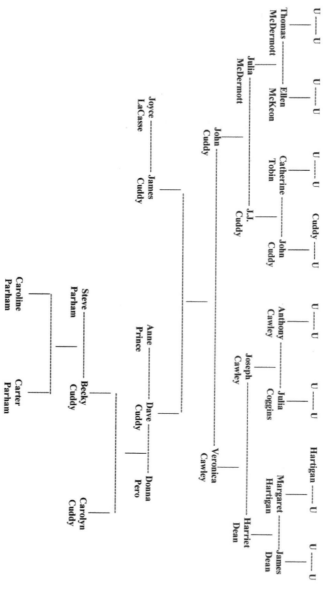

U = Unknown

Chapter One

First Generation:
Famine Generation, c. 1820

"Other forms were near. His soul had approached that region where dwell the vast hosts of the dead. He was conscious of, but could not apprehend, their wayward and flickering existence."

James Joyce, "The Dead" from The Dubliners

Designated Family Storyteller

Like the designated hitter in baseball, I'm the designated family storyteller. But I never expected that a trip back to my ancestral land of Ireland would widen my role to story writer. When I gathered family stories, I was surprised by my clan's involvement in the sweep of historical events from the Irish Potato Famine, to the U.S. Civil War, to the disruption of a Ku Klux Klan Parade. Our family experienced vocational changes from blacksmithing, to shoe manufacturing, to administrating at IBM.

"Jim, I'm handing on to you my role of family storyteller," aged Aunt Jule Cawley said to me, in 1993. She was visibly relieved to be free of this responsibility. "You know the key family stories, and I've given you many photos, but my Bible has pages with vital statistics. When I die, be sure to get those important dates."

And so I became the storyteller – 'seanachie' in Gaelic. There was no clap of thunder, no ceremony with the tapping of my shoulder with a shillelagh, no solemn spelling out of rights and duties. After Aunt Jule's funeral, a cousin made copies of the priceless data pages from the family Bible for me. By this book of stories, I have kept faith with Aunt Jule and our family through seven generations from the Irish Famine to the present day.

In compiling family stories, I found that each successive generation left more documents and photos. Before Dad died, he researched our family tree, and I can read my weak copy by squinting under good light. I also relied on my own memories. In my sixty-seven years, I've vividly seen a myriad of family events and clearly heard a multitude of family conversations. In addition, I glimpsed shadowy scenes that clarified over time and overheard whispered words that made sense to me later. Like a woodsman honing his ax, I carefully sharpened my skill of reading between the lines of family developments. For the record, I readily confess that some family events, memories, and yarns remain unsolved for me. I am no Sherlock Holmes, able to solve every family mystery.

My fourteen-month older and only sibling Dave and I perceived some family stories differently.

"Your stories are like van Gogh's paintings with bright colors," he said to me in mid-life.

"Well, you're at times like Rembrandt with darker paints and shadows," I said.

Dave and I differed about some memories and stories, but not about the essentials of our boyhood. Like Huck Finn and Tom Sawyer we were mischievous, not on the Mississippi, but along the Susquehanna River in Endicott, New York. We saw, heard, smelled, tasted, and touched the same realities when growing up, but interpreted them through the filters of our own personalities. Each felt that his stories were correct, but in time we realized the truth was probably in the middle.

Like most families, ours told its stories not as strict history, but as voices heard, events seen, emotions felt viscerally. Our family stories were organic and changed in the telling and re-telling. My father embellished his yarns, my mother sanitized her tales, and, as indicated, Dave darkened his accounts, and I lightened mine. But in this book I'm not a historian, genealogist, or autobiographer. I am simply the family storyteller.

Back to the Ancestral Homeland

To find background for the first generation, which I call the Famine Generation, my wife Joyce and I toured Ireland in 1999. Our aim was to hike to the mountain source of our family's name and to visit Irish Famine memorials. A successful climb to the peak of Mount Everest, the top of the world, makes an international statement, and a trek to Mt. McKinley, the summit of North America, makes a continental statement. My planned hike to Carrantuohill, the highest point in MacGillycuddy's Reeks and the summit of all Ireland, would make an Irish and family statement. My name Cuddy is the rump cut of MacGillycuddy, and I had the lofty goal of reaching the top of The Reeks and validating my family roots. This was my third visit to Ireland and Joyce's first.

The day before the ascent Joyce and I parked on a remote road in County Kerry and tiptoed through the cow chips in a pasture to a spot for a panoramic photo of the distant Reeks. While looking at the peak, I felt a shiver cross my back from right shoulder to left; I sensed that something enchanted awaited me on the top.

"What beauty!" Joyce said. I nodded and sized up the mountain that I was determined to climb. The peak was 3,414 feet high, but because the starting point wasn't far above sea level, it would be a long and hard trek up and down in one day.

An ancient man with a rakishly cocked hat suddenly stepped out of the hedgerow. He studied us while we took his measure. His face was like the map of Ireland, with left eye peering from Dublin and right eye squinting from Galway. His nose was the Rock of Cashel in the midlands, and his wry smile the crooked, west-to-east Killarney to Dungarvan road.

"My name's Jim Cuddy, from MacGillycuddy. We've come from America to hike up to the top of MacGillycuddy's Reeks," I said. "This is my wife Joyce." He bowed to her with a half-bow.

"It's a long way up, and some don't make the summit. I'm a local seanachie or storyteller according to you Yanks," he said with a heavy brogue, extending his hand to me, gnarled like the roots of an oak.

"Jim's seanachie for our family," Joyce said. "He tells stories from seven generations."

"Do you really have such a long chain of relatives and stories?" he said, with no effort to conceal his skepticism. I was a suspicious, foreign seanachie on his turf.

"I do. I do from the famine generation through six generations of increasing plenty in America. I'll spare you the several family pictures in my wallet," I said, patting my wallet pocket threateningly, like a gunfighter touching his gun in a western movie. If he reached for his wallet pictures, I would quick-draw mine first.

"You're the first Yank in a while not to show pictures," he said. "I've known those with your family name, long and short, a mountainy people. Many went to America." So thick was his brogue that I couldn't get his name despite three attempts. As we tried to communicate, I realized that he used a Gaelic form for my longer family name that sounded like "MacGillacudda" with accents on the second and fourth syllables. I'll use his form as the authentic pronunciation with my best guess for the spelling. When I deciphered his request for a ride to Killorglin, I winced. Our tiny rental car was cluttered with loose clothes and luggage.

"Can you take him to nearby Killorglin and then come back for me?" I said to Joyce.

"Wouldn't it be easier if you came with us?" she said, raising her right eyebrow in a coded message of wariness. "Try sliding over some clothes on the back seat."

While he talked with Joyce up front, I smelled the strong, but not unpleasant, odor of the peat fire from his clothes. "Will you be in Killorglin in August for Puck Fair?" he said to her, promoting his corner of Ireland. We began to understand his accent more easily and vice versa.

"No, we're here only for June. Is that a special time?" Joyce said, warming up to him.

"Pity, we enthrone a goat with ribbons in its horns and celebrate for three days. Some say it goes back to magical pre-Christian days. You must return someday and attend Puck Fair."

When we dropped him off in Killorglin, he invited us for a drink, but we declined because we had a dinner reservation in Killarney. After I helped him to the sidewalk, I pressed a fiver in his hand. He smiled with teeth like a broken picket fence, winked his thanks, and bowed with a quarter-bow. When I got back to the car, I turned to wave, but he had vanished.

"You haven't said a word since Killorglin," said Joyce, as we entered Killarney.

"That seanachie might've been a benign friend-of-the-family spirit. He appeared suddenly and disappeared quickly," I said whimsically, ever the poet in our marriage. "He was welcoming us to The Reeks. Don't you see? I should've asked him more about our family ancestors."

"I wish I could share your penchant for spirits," Joyce said, always the realist, keeping me grounded. "Having seen The Reeks from a distance, I've decided to stroll and shop in

Killarney tomorrow rather than join you in such a long trek. Our hike up Croagh Patrick last week was enough for me."

A week earlier, in mid-June we shared a hike at Croagh Patrick in County Mayo. Each year on the last Sunday of July, thousands of pilgrims, a few with penitentially bare feet, have climbed the mountain to the chapel of Saint Patrick on the summit. Although Croagh Patrick is shorter and more compact than MacGillycuddy's Reeks, Joyce and I found that the hike was a difficult five hour round-trip. Once on top, hail whitened our hats, but then the clouds lifted, and the unimpeded view – most mountains in Ireland are treeless from top to bottom – was breathtaking. Looking one way, we could see peaks in Connemara and in another direction, Clew Bay.

We noticed that a young couple, the male with bare feet, arrived at the summit.

"I hiked the rocky top section without boots to show solidarity with my rugged ancestors rather than to perform a penitential act," he replied to my why. Carrying his boots over her hands like boxing gloves, his girlfriend looked bewildered as if she had just discovered a new side to her boyo and wasn't sure he was the right one for marriage and fathering her children.

Validating Roots ~ MacGillycuddy's Reeks

Eight days after Croagh Patrick and one day after the friend-of-the-family spirit, I drove to a remote valley to hike up Carrantuohill, the tip of The Reeks and of all Ireland. The three sections of trail were bogs, pastures, and rocks. Beyond the soggy bogs, many sheep, like teens that I've taught, gave me utterly bored and vacant looks. I joined four English hikers for a rest and brief visit. Their accent was thicker than Hadrian's Wall in England, and I realized later that my upstate New York accent was probably heavier than an American tourist's guidebook to them.

Left, right, left. Hike, left, up. More hike, left, hike. More up, up, up. Over the second highest Irish mountain, Cahir, I trudged. Four hours into my climb, as I wearily and warily – I had a premonition of something unusual on top – neared the rocky summit of MacGillycuddy's Reeks, I saw the dramatic steel cross at the summit. Clouds, flying off the Atlantic and briefly shaking out light hail, blew in with eerie suddenness. Alone at the peak, I was sore, sweaty, and salted with hail, but also exhilarated enough to dance a brief victory jig. After I touched the steel cross, I offered a prayer to the God who fashioned mountains for our awe. I slumped against a large rock, closed my eyes, and felt the satisfaction of those who, singly or in teams, conquered mountains.

For a minute I heard or thought I heard faint Irish music with uilleann pipes and bodhran drums, followed by singing and laughter. Was I asleep or awake? Looking around and seeing no one, I felt my neck hairs standing at attention. Did I hear the Cuddy or MacGillacudda spirits making enchanted music and song? Did I touch the religious world? Perhaps I experienced in a heightened way favorite lines from James Joyce: "Other forms were near. His soul had approached that region where dwell the vast hosts of the dead."

The musicmakers probably were ancestral spirits. I wanted to know whether my encounter was an enchanted, religious, or heightened literary experience, but decided to accept the occurrence without instant analysis. Fear gave way to joy and peace as I realized I had validated my roots in a surprising way. I strained to hear more, but silence now ruled the peak. Then the clouds lifted verifying the Irish weather's reputation for quick changes like the moods of surly then sunny teenagers.

The English hikers, breaking my mystical mood, arrived at the summit. One of them, using my camera, took my picture on the top of The Reeks. Concentrating again, I found the views liberating to my soul; mountain peaks always prompted prayers of thanksgiving in me. I wondered whether van Gogh would've loved the mountains and glens of Kerry with their soft and magical light. Then I imagined that the MacGillacuddas down below must be a hearty stock. I wanted to stay longer in case my family spirits sang again, but I had thousands of steps to retrace.

As a mountain hiker, I've trekked in fifteen American states and once reached the top of Pikes Peak, over 14,000 feet tall, from which I happily took the tourist train down. From these varied hikes, I found trudging down mountains to be anticlimactic and punishing to the knees. To pass time on descents, hiking friends and I've talked about silly topics. To keep myself occupied on this descent, I mentally listed my ancestors. I knew my parents and three grandparents well, and I had stories about four of my eight great-grandparents, but only a picture of one great-great-grandparent. These and most other forerunners had Irish surnames according to Dad's family tree.

Left, right, left, right, left. Picking my way down the rocky section, I relived my experience of singing spirits. This triggered a witch's brew of stories to bubble up in my memory, in random order, about my parents, grandparents, and great-grandparents, and with imaginings about my great-great-grandparents. I suddenly felt compelled to do more than tell family stories; I sensed the empowerment to write the tales of four generations. Left, write, left, write. But what about the fifth generation of my brother and me? What about my two nieces of the sixth generation? What about the seventh generation of my grandniece and grandnephew? I stopped, pondered at length, and decided then and there, as family storyteller, to undertake the mission to write stories about all seven generations. Write, left, write, left, write.

For years I had interest in literary family tales. I enjoyed Frank McCourt's stories in *Angela's Ashes*. He was like an alchemist to me, spinning filaments of gold from his base family yarns. I much admired his clever and darkly humorous style. Write, left, write, left, aspire to alchemy. I heard "baaaa, baaaa, baaaa, ba," as three sheep and one ewe crossed my path. Their languor, their lassitude, their listlessness did little to urge me on.

After a longer rest, I slogged down the boggy section. Squish, splash, "squoosh," "squesh," "splush," "sploosh." I wondered whether James Joyce, with his gift for coining words, had hiked to exhaustion in his early days and made up words in that state.

Beyond the final knoll, I saw the rental car and pressed myself to a quicker pace with a whispered cadence of themes used directly by Homer in *The Odyssey* and later indirectly by James Joyce in *Ulysses*. I started this way: left, right, Calypso,

Hades, Wandering Rocks, Sirens, Cyclops, Penelope. Soon I jumbled the cadence. It ended at the car something like this: Calypso Beat, Heyday, Rock Music, Police Sirens, One-Eyed Jack, Penny. At any rate, I completed my trek with a mental and physical flourish.

My ascent took about four hours and the descent almost five. In 1999, at sixty-two, I took longer to go down mountains than up them. I was glad my family name wasn't McKinley. With or without guides, I couldn't climb vast and snowy Mount McKinley in Alaska. After a nap with my bootless feet sticking out of the small car's window, I drove from the magical Reeks to join Joyce and her realism in Killarney.

"I've a powerful thirst after my long trek," I said to her from the lobby phone; I was too tired even for the elevator. "My throat is caked with trail dust, bog pollen, and sheep dust. And I heard some ancestral spirits singing. Will you join me for a pint of porter and some pub grub?"

"I'll be down in a few minutes. I had a great time walking and shopping," she said. "I'm eager to hear about your trek to the top of The Reeks," she paused, "and yes, those singing spirits."

A pint of Guinness was temporarily curative of my fatigue, but I knew that the next day every muscle and bone would ache. I listened to Joyce's stories about shopping and strolling around scenic Killarney. She then heard about my adventurous hike up and down MacGillycuddy's Reeks. I told her about singing family spirits and concluded that I experienced a combined enchanted-religious-literary phenomenon to which I added a pinch of whimsy. "I believe that eternal life begins on earth, but fully transforms individuals, families, and other social groups in the hereafter," I said. "I heard a preview."

"However you describe the experience, I support your quest for family roots," Joyce said, touching my hand affectionately.

Before we left the pub, I noticed a small scene about a difference in accents. Some of life's little joys are seen out of the corner of one's eye. Our lovely waitress spoke to us with a perfect Oxford accent. I described to Joyce my fanciful impression of the waitress, "She goes from table to table gracefully, like a salmon slithering – no snakes need apply in Ireland. And her voice reminds me of Audrey Hepburn, after her linguistic transformation in the movie *My Fair Lady*." Joyce agreed with my assessment. Two boyos in old-sod stained soccer uniforms came in and sat near us. I nudged Joyce, and we watched. They listened to the Oxford accent of the attractive waitress and gave their orders in heavy Kerry brogue. As she left their table, both looked away and sighed.

What is the concern of Americans and others for their Irish roots? Why vacations in tiny cars on narrow roads in Ireland? I can't fully explain it. I think I had been secretly hoping for family spirits to validate my roots, and my hope was fulfilled on top of The Reeks. And I believe that on some distant day Joyce and I will be on The Reeks in our spirit state with my ancestors to welcome Cuddys, MacGillacuddas, MacGillycuddys, Codys, Quiddys Cuddahays, Cuddahies, MacGills, Gills, and others with long or short forms of our family name when they come home again by validating hikes or by death. I further believe that we'll also welcome Joyce's French-Canadian-American spirit-relatives with LaCasse, Marois, and other French names on some high peak in Quebec or France, but that is another book of stories, perhaps from Dane LaCasse, computerized record keeper on Joyce's side of the family.

Working back from the time of the known second generation in America to the almost unknown first generation in Ireland, I presumed that my early ancestors, Dad's MacGillacuddas and Mom's Hartigans, had fled the Famine. They escaped from hunger to a land of hope, plenty, and freedom. My ancestors fled from Ireland as many others did from their countries. All refugees escape something different, but they have the same high hopes. Millions of immigrants saw America as their refuge, and they are still coming.

Famine Memorials ~ Coffin Ships and Sinuous Art

The 150th Anniversary of the Irish Famine, in 1995, prompted several harrowing books and other remembrances. During our time in Ireland, Joyce and I visited two thought-provoking and grim Irish Famine memorials for background information. The Famine Memorial at the foot of Croagh Patrick in County Mayo was striking. The large outdoor sculpture of a sailing ship drew us into its meaning. Riggings of the ship were elongated skeletons to depict the many deaths at sea in aptly named "coffin ships." The hardships of crossing the Atlantic in small ships caused the deaths of many half-starved refugees. Some estimated that 1.5 million Irish died, on land and sea, in the catastrophic Irish Famine in 1845 and following years, and that 1.5 million Irish fled their country to safety. The horror of the Famine may help to explain a melancholy streak in some Irish. All that hunger and all those corpses – how did they bury so many bodies? – must've affected our collective psyche and may be one factor in understanding alcohol abuse among some Irish and Irish-Americans.

The Queenstown Story Center in County Cork was another place for us to brood. A multimedia journey into the past captured the sadness of those fleeing the Famine, and a sculpture depicted a mother looking back to Ireland and the past, while her older child pointed west toward America and the future. I was amazed that my forerunners survived at all with so many odds against them, and I felt that I inexplicably survived with them or in them. They came over the sea to a world unknown to them and made it the only world known to their future descendants.

Even though I come from Irish and Catholic background, our family saga is not only for the Irish-Catholics. Our story can be transposed to any family of any ethnic or racial background. Similarly in 1977, the TV miniseries *Roots* was enormously popular for that reason. Though it told the story of one black family from Africa to America through several generations, it spoke to many people on different levels. Author Alex Haley was able to write in universal terms, and the show was appreciated by all, not just those of African descent.

Wandering through the exhibits, I tried to interpret the 154 years from the Famine to our return in 1999. I finally imagined three bronze vessels – an Irish stew pot, a pot-of-gold, and a melting pot. All were decorated with sinuous Celtic art. Greek and Roman artists favored straight lines in art, but the

Celts preferred the curve in their swirly, flowing, and convoluted art. The three artistic vessels gradually suggested their meanings to me. Dad's MacGillacuddas and Mom's Hartigans probably fled the Famine and sought an Irish stew pot with something to eat, anything to eat. From records and experience, I knew that subsequent generations of our family pursued the pot-of-gold at the end of the American economic rainbow, and Dave and I experienced the melting pot of public and parochial schools to a hot degree. I wish my ancestors could see how their primitive longings for food led to the more complex desires of the subsequent generations. We have evolved from Irish in Ireland, to Irish in America, to Americans with Irish background.

During three trips to Ireland, I enjoyed stays of two or three days with a lovely family, the O'Mahonys in tiny Ballinacurra, County Cork. Their ancestors did not flee Ireland, but somehow survived the Famine years. During the last visit, "Cousin" Ursula took Joyce and me on a scenic tour of eastern County Cork that included the small fishing town Ballycotton, and she ended her tour at the ancient St. Colman's Cathedral, which dated back to the year 1250, in the rural village Cloyne. I marveled at the list of successive bishops of Cloyne, covering two high cathedral walls. Our United States history is relatively short in comparison with the centuries and centuries of Irish artifacts, records, and ruins.

Highlights of Ireland Tour

As Joyce and I took off from Shannon Airport, I remembered that on two prior return flights to America, Aer Lingus planes followed the Shannon River to the Atlantic Ocean and flew on to Boston. This time the weather conditions were clear, and I could see from the plane's window beyond Dingle Peninsula to MacGillycuddy's Reeks, capped by a single ivory cloud. I wondered whether I would ever climb The Reeks again, or visit Puck Fair for the first time, or chat again with the friend-of-the-family spirit-seanachie. Memories filled my mind of our month-long self-tour along the seacoast of Ireland and in Dublin, and I tried to rank my memories from best to great to good. I placed a few recollections in a mental column earmarked for negatives.

"A big Irish copper or tuppence for your thoughts," Joyce whispered.

"I was thinking of my best memory – hiking up The Reeks in County Kerry and the music at the summit. And I was looking forward to my mission to write generational stories," I said, while eating airline peanuts one at a time. "What are your best memories of Ireland?"

"I especially enjoyed the bed and breakfasts, twelve homes and eighteen nights by my notes, not including the hotels. Remember the host who put Bailey's Irish Cream in my morning oatmeal and smoked salmon in your eggs?"

"I remember. I remember. And I enjoyed ocean fishing near Kilmore Quay in Wexford."

"Next for me was watching razorbills and puffins on Great Saltee Island in that same area," she said. "A beautiful side tour."

"I liked Trinity College and that street sculpture of James Joyce in Dublin. I enjoyed our several days in Dublin and clearly sensed their 'Celtic Tiger' booming economy. They definitely have a tiger by the tail."

"I loved the play *Dancing at Lughnasa* at the Abbey Theater in Dublin," said Joyce, "even more than the movie version with Meryl Streep."

"Remote Achill Island in County Donegal was sparsely settled and starkly attractive, and I recall Keem Beach and the narrow cliff road that seemed to lead, not to the end of the island, but to the end of the world," I said, concluding my positives of our month's tour. "But in my negative column, I would put the need for workers and residents to pick up the litter in cities and villages, especially in Dublin."

"And they could widen their roads for greater safety," she added a negative, "especially in ocean and farm areas where driving was a challenge. The road over Connor Pass in Dingle was the most threatening with the fog and narrow roadway, and I had only inches to spare when a van from the opposite direction crept slowly by us. I'm glad that tour buses are not allowed to use the pass."

A late arrival positive memory. "I liked sheep on the roadway. I found wisps of wool on the sides of the car several times from your driving so close to the sheep," I said, pulling her leg. Riding on the left side of the car, I often gasped when I felt Joyce was about to scrape stone walls that closely lined narrow roads, but Joyce is a good driver and navigated the narrow roads and streets well.

"Amen, to a great vacation," Joyce said and settled back in the adjustable seat.

"Amen," I echoed.

As the plane droned across the wide Atlantic, I wondered how family spirits cross the sea. I recalled that Frank McCourt raised a similar question in *Angela's Ashes*: "I sit at the graves of Oliver and Eugene in the old St. Patrick's Burying Ground and cross the road to St. Lawrence's Cemetery where Theresa is buried. Wherever I go I hear voices of the dead and I wonder if they can follow you across the Atlantic Ocean."

After wrestling with this question at length and bouncing playful ideas off Joyce at home, I concluded that family ghosts travel back and forth across the Atlantic not in empty seats on Aer Lingus airplanes, but by their own spirit power. This was my lighthearted guess, and I'm glad Frank McCourt raised the issue for debate by his readers. Some religious questions are best left to storytellers, poets, and creative writers rather than to serious scholars of religion. The Catholic religion can be heavy and dour if we forget the humor, joy, and laughter sprinkled in the gospels of the Bible and in our traditions.

Sizing Up the Mission to Write

Memories of the singing spirits on The Reeks energized me to evaluate many boxes of family records and photos from the back of my closet. I was amazed at the quantity and quality of the family records. By hard work, I knew that I could fulfill my commitment to write stories about seven generations. I also recognized most of the relatives and friends in the hundreds of photos and decided to place strictly limited pictures at the end of each chapter to sum up the feeling and flow of each generation. On a few occasions, I placed a photo in the middle of a chapter for emphasis and clarity.

Everyone has to conclude the official genealogical search somewhere, beyond which lie dragons of imagination, and I had ended my formal search in America. Reading about Irish heraldry prompted my informal search for general family roots in Ireland. I discovered that the Cuddy name was tied to MacGillycuddy's Reeks, depicted at the top of our coat-of-arms. I presumed that Mom's relatives, the Hartigans, were also from Kerry. Most marriages in rural and mountain areas were between people from the same county. The next family storyteller can pursue computerized genealogy in Ireland, America, and elsewhere with my blessing. I plan to designate niece Becky of the sixth generation to replace me.

Because the earliest generation was mostly beyond my reach into the distant past, I had to imagine details. For these sections I've carefully used "I presumed," "I believed," "they probably," "they must have," or the equivalent to alert the reader. To make the first generation on my mother's side more real, let's imagine that Great-great-grandmother Hartigan (first and maiden names unknown) married farmer Hartigan in about 1840. They probably farmed near Killarney with a few sheep, a cow, and a subsistence crop of potatoes. Theirs would have been a tenant farm, and most of the yield went to the landlord. There was little margin for error in such a primitive economy, as the Irish Famine made clear when the potato blight struck in successive years. The Hartigans and the MacGillacuddas might've escaped catastrophic Ireland by sailing to America from Galway, around "Black '47," the bottom of the pit of the Famine.

"Does our family warrant a book with stories from seven generations?" Joyce said, when she saw my absorption in organizing, outlining, and writing family stories, months after Ireland.

"Well on the one hand, we're ordinary people, but on the other hand I have unusual stories about the U.S. Civil War, an Irish wake, the breakup of the Ku Klux Klan parade," I said and paused to think of more key stories. "And a family ghost story, bittersweet tales of the Depression, childhood yarns from Dave and me about World War II, the Holocaust seen on newsreels, light and reflective tales from when I was a parish priest. And you know the best modern stories."

"And your voice for this book? Have you finally settled on your voice?" she asked, from her experience as an avid reader.

"I gradually developed my voice to blend lighthearted and serious melodies. This voice I modeled on my Grandfather and Grandmother Cawley. Both spoke seriously about family tales, but more often they reminisced with light wit and a subtle smile. I can still hear in my memory how they talked and I made their voices my own for this book."

"I'm curious, how did you begin?" she asked. "And then no more questions today."

"While the Famine generation is sketchy, I have this special picture as a key to the first generation," I said, handing to her a four-generation photo that showed my Great-great-grandmother Hartigan with three younger ancestors, the youngest of which was my mother.

"It's easy to see that the toddler in the photo was your mother."

"Families should take four-generation pictures whenever they can. They are rarities."

After studying the minimal data of our first generation, I made this detailed family layout.

Paternal Side/MacGillacuddas	Maternal Side/Hartigans
Seven great-great-grandparents unknown.	Six great-great-grandparents: unknown.
One of the great-great-grandparents had to carry the Cuddy name, but no records until the second generation.	One great-great-grandfather Hartigan, only his last name known.
	One great-great-grandmother Hartigan, her maiden name unknown, oldest one in four-generation picture.

Four-generation photo of maternal side, counterclockwise from right: Great-great-grandmother Hartigan (1st generation), Great-grandmother Margaret Hartigan Dean (2nd gen.), Grandmother Harriet Dean Cawley (3rd gen.), Veronica Cawley (later Mom Cuddy, 4th gen.) as toddler in 1908.

In this four-generation family picture of the maternal side of our family, Great-great-grandmother Hartigan wore a dark dress with bow and veil, which is still seen in southwest Ireland. In contrast to this traditional dress, Great-grandma Dean modeled a dramatic hat, and Grandmother Cawley and Mom reflected stylish attire of 1908. The oldest ancestor held my mother's hand to complete the circle of life. Her ancient face was kind, and her hands were wrinkled from age and work. These details were all I could glean from the picture of this first-generation forerunner. This priceless photo touched my soul, and brother Dave, similarly affected, hung a large copy of this photo in his den.

In a collection of her interviews, Toni Morrison, author of *Paradise* and other works, told of four generations of her family in one room. Ms. Morrison's profound reaction to this scene was similar to the mystical impact of our family's four-generation photo on Dave and me.

Multicultural Inspiration From Experts

Once I began writing family stories, I found help in many books. Retirement years gave me time to browse in bookstores and libraries. Like a deer in luxurious meadows, I browsed with freedom and delight. I discovered Calvin Trillin's *Messages from My Father* wherein he celebrates the humor of Jewish family stories in the Midwest. Martha Manning's *Chasing Grace, Reflections of a Catholic Girl, Grown Up* gives a girl's-eye view of growing up Catholic, as I was writing my boy's-eye view. I also valued the humorous works of Garrison Keillor, professional storyteller, about life with unusual and Protestant characters in his fictional world of Lake Wobegon, Minnesota. Elie Wiesel, in the tales of Hasidic masters in *Souls on Fire*, shares powerful insights into Jewish family storytelling.

In addition, I valued Russell Baker's "russdrollery," which I coined to indicate the droll wit and wise writing found in Mr. Baker's books and columns. In *Growing Up*, Russell Baker crystallized the value of family stories for me: "We all come from the past, and children ought to know what it was that went into their making, to know that life is a braided cord of humanity stretching up from time long gone, and that it cannot be defined by the span of a single journey from diaper to shroud."

I was brash enough to approach Russell Baker by mail for advice about the first draft of this book. I now cringe at the quality of that early version; perhaps sixty percent of this book has changed since that primitive form. Although Mr. Baker didn't have time to comment on the text, he sent a personal letter with valuable support: "What I must tell you is that the important thing you have done is to assemble all this material about your family. Your progeny will bless you for it in years to come. So few families have any record keepers, and those who keep the records do a priceless service to their families-to-be." In a similar way, Aunt Jule saw the value of family tales, photos, and records when she designated me as family storyteller.

Perhaps some readers, whether designated or not, will take up the roles of record keeper, storyteller, and even story writer of their family sagas. To encourage others, I wove into my text, especially in this first chapter, suggested ways and means for writing family stories. In the Appendix, I also shared formal hints, ten in all, for the how-to of writing family tales. Niece Becky, my successor and seanachie-in-waiting, can designate either Caroline or Carter Parham of the seventh generation to update this book with stories to reflect his or her complex (Irish-Italian-Scots Irish etc.) family tree. The official storyteller of the seventh generation can in turn designate a successor to keep the process going into the twenty-second century.

I resonated with the long historical view of storytelling. Time gradually changed the ancient storytelling process from oral to written form. Modern families no longer tell their stories around an outdoor fire beneath the canopy of stars. Central heating, television, and home computers have changed all that. Going with the flow of history, I've written down our family stories for relatives and general readers to enjoy in or on lounge chairs, beds, bathtubs, subways, jet planes, beaches in summer, and ski lodges in winter.

In the next chapter, the call of the trumpet and the drumbeat of the U.S. Civil War will be heard in the land. I'll introduce a fifteen year-old Irish-American boy, James Dean, who answered the call and served in the Union Army, and I'll tell of a skilled laborer, Anthony Cawley, who was a pioneer of Endicott, New York.

"…I found the views liberating to my soul."
Jim on summit with the second highest peak behind him, 1999.

"However you describe the experience, I support your quest for family roots." Joyce on the scenic Ring of Kerry, 1999.

"Riggings of the ship were elongated skeletons to depict
the many deaths at sea in aptly named 'coffin ships.'"
Sculpture at Famine Memorial at foot of Croagh Patrick, 1999.

"…and a sculpture depicted a mother looking back to Ireland and
the past, while her older child pointed west toward America and
the future." A silhouette photo at Queenstown Story Center in
Cork, 1999.

Chapter Two

Second Generation:
U.S. Civil War Generation, 1845

*"We tend to think of memory as a camera, or a
tape recorder, where the past can be filed intact
and called up at will. But memory is none of these
things. Memory is a storyteller, and like all storytellers
it imposes form on the raw mass of experience. It
creates shape and meaning by emphasizing some
things and leaving others out. It finds connections
between events, suggests cause and effect."*

Tobias Wolfe, New York Times Digest

Second Generation: Eight Great-grandparents

Paternal Side   Maternal Side

John Cuddy   Anthony Cawley
Catherine Tobin   Julia Coggins

Thomas McDermott   James Dean
Ellen McKeon   Margaret Hartigan

I've never been called a mick fondly or disparagingly. Two of my eight great-grandparents were literally micks, namely McDermott and McKeon, and I've already noted that Cuddy came from the longer MacGillacudda. All eight – micks, macks, and others – were probably born around 1845. The four families of this generation had thirty-three children, of whom all but seven had married, according to Dad's family tree. Much of their social lives must've been taken up with planning and coordinating twenty-six marriage celebrations.

My ancestors lived in Pennsylvania in an arc from Pottsville to Wilkes-Barre to Carbondale. Our family was like a 150-mile vein of hard coal that surfaced along this line. Of those in the second generation, I have stories about James Dean, Margaret Hartigan Dean, Anthony Cawley, and Thomas McDermott. I only have a picture of Ellen McKeon McDermott.

Great-Grandfather James Dean ~ Civil War Soldier

James Dean, born in 1847, joined the Union Army at fifteen to fight in the Civil War. He faced combat at Gettysburg, where casualties were heavy on both sides. I wish I had detailed war stories to tell, but I don't. Fortunate to have survived the fighting, he was discharged at eighteen in Philadelphia. He probably took a train to Scranton and a stagecoach to the town nearest his home. I imagined the joyful reunion when he walked up the road to his farm home with his war rifle slung casually across his shoulder.

Faded (often copied over the years) September 6, 1865 Discharge Certificate of Corporal James Dean from the Union Army. He served from age fifteen to eighteen.

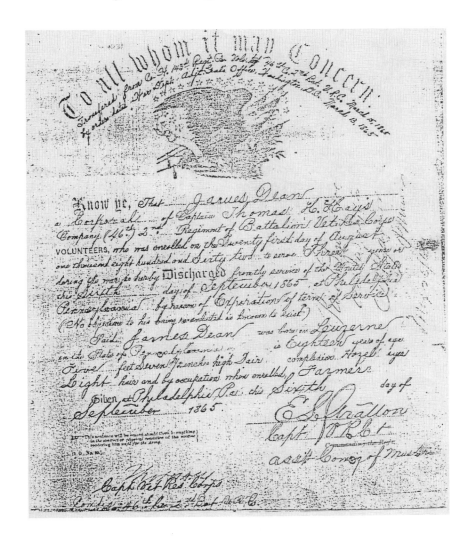

Holding his Civil War discharge certificate to the window and alternating the close and far lenses of my bifocals, I discovered these facts about James Dean:
- rank of Corporal, Co. H., 143rd Regt., Pa. Volunteers
- enrolled on August 1, 1862 and discharged on September 6, 1865, at age eighteen
- born in Leuzerne (sic) County in Pennsylvania
- five feet and seven & 1/2 inches high, fair complexion, hazel eyes, light hair, and farmer.

Decades ago brother Dave became a Civil War buff and grasped the importance of this discharge record. I had thought of it as vaguely interesting, but later realized it was the earliest documentary evidence of the second generation. Dave also searched until he found the name James Dean listed as a survivor on the enormous Pennsylvania Memorial at Gettysburg.

"Corporal James Dean was my father, and this was his Civil War rifle," Grandma Harriet Dean Cawley said to Dave and me when we were boys. She kept the rusty and disintegrating relic in her garage; it could not be fired and was not a danger to anyone. Grandma let us hold the eighty-plus-year-old rifle, and we studied it with awe and admiration. In the bottom of a box of photos, I recently found a picture of young Dave with the long Civil War rifle over his shoulder. This picture confirmed my memory of the family relic.

I presume other relatives, besides Corporal James Dean, fought in the Union Army in the Civil War. The Irish and Irish-Americans were well represented because immigrants generally wanted to demonstrate allegiance to their new country. "In all, as many as 150,000 Union soldiers were Irish-born – up to 51,000 from New York State alone – and thousands more were of Irish parentage," wrote Ann Kathleen Bradley in her *History of the Irish in America*.

Four generations after the Civil War niece Becky Cuddy married Steve Parham, who is from a long line of southern families. I've wondered whether Corporal James Dean of the Pennsylvania Volunteers fought against Steve's ancestors at Gettysburg. When cast in personal and family terms, reflections on the madness of war are depressing for me. All wars are horrible and destructive, but civil wars are the worst kind.

Let's presume that the Hartigans of the Famine generation landed safely in New York and then settled in northeastern Pennsylvania where the Irish worked on railroads, farms, and in coalmines. Our family records began in this era. Margaret Hartigan, born in 1850, married James Dean. At this point the Hartigan name was absorbed by the Dean name. The hardscrabble land was as resistant to the plow as the rocky fields in parts of County Kerry, but the Deans must've been happy to be alive with a full Irish stew pot and the chance to pursue the pot-of-gold of economic growth. They probably told handed-down stories of the mountains, magical light, and stark beauty of County Kerry. The Deans eventually moved from Pennsylvania across the state line to a farm on a high hill, ten miles south of what soon became Endicott, New York.

A caption on a later family photo called the Dean farm "Mount Joy." However, farm life was demanding for all family members and isolating from neighbors. Harriet Dean, one of the eleven children of James Dean and Margaret Hartigan, and later my Grandmother Cawley told me that rural life, despite her large family, was too lonely for her. She said, "I sometimes walked the long road from our farm to town to visit friends because I was lonesome."

Ghost stories were part of our family's lore. Once when Grandma Dean Cawley was telling a ghost story, I winked at Dave – we were in our twenties – and we snickered. She later rebuked me for my impolite and incredulous attitude. I don't know whether she cornered, confronted, and chastised Dave. I generally held a skeptical attitude toward ghosts, but in the last decade I developed a playful penchant for spirits, which was confirmed by my enchanted-religious-literary encounter with family spirits on the Kerry Reeks. The Irish speak of "thin places" when talking about the closeness of the spirit world to us. An example follows.

"When I was a teenager, I went out to our farm's well to draw a bucket of water for washing dishes," Grandma Cawley said, relishing center stage. "After I drew the water, I saw a ghost sitting near the well, smoking his pipe. Terrified, I dropped the bucket and ran back to the house with the dreadful news. Dad grabbed his Civil War rifle and rushed out, but didn't see any ghost." To her it was a vivid, if brief, experience. Her face was fully animated, and she expected everyone to believe her tale. I've long maintained that the story probably began as a tall tale by a lonely farm teen seeking attention and excitement, but I heard her tell it so often, two generations later, that I realized it was real to her.

I've since imagined a richer version. In my more emotionally charged story, Corporal James Dean, veteran of the Pennsylvania Volunteers and hardened by years of farming, would've brandished his Civil War rifle and then run the ghost off his land with a warning shot. James Dean would've been heroic, even Homeric, one not to be trifled with by man, woman, beast, or ghost.

There were some formal attempts to settle Irish immigrants on the land in America rather than in poor, crowded, and urban neighborhoods. One of these experiments was in northeastern Pennsylvania, near the New York border. I read that the land proved to be too rocky, and only some of the Irish settlers thrived by farming. Many of these Irish families eventually moved across the state line to the urban area of Binghamton, New York to find factory work.

I recalled friends telling of their country roots "out our way," as they called the Irish farm area. Tom Cawley, a columnist for the *Binghamton Press*, (Aunt Jule Cawley corresponded with him and found that he was not a relative of our family), for years wrote his human interest pieces under the title: "Out Our Way." I also listened to stories of our family's early farm life and never heard accounts to suggest that my relatives were part of the formal farm experiment. The Dean branch of our family finally gave up farming and moved to Endicott.

I have a naming story that goes back to tales by my mother. When I was born in 1936, Mom suggested that I be named in honor of her Grandfather James Dean. "Let's call him James Dean Cuddy. You know about Corporal James Dean."

"Wait a minute. Are you sure this is a good idea?" Dad protested. "Most people won't know the Dean background. It will sound like he has two last names. What if we compromise? How about just James?" he suggested, and Mom agreed. I sometimes wished they had concurred on James Dean Cuddy. I would've liked sharing a name in part with movie actor James Dean. Dave may have been named for Mom's relative David Dean, but I don't recall asking her for details about Dave's name – a lost opportunity.

Great-Grandmother Margaret Hartigan Dean ~ Benign Matriarch

Great-grandmother Margaret Hartigan Dean wore a dramatic hat in the previous four-generation picture. I picked up her story after she survived the death of husband James Dean. Mom described her as warm and friendly, a benign matriarch. Her home, at the corner of North Street and Lincoln Avenue in Endicott, was the family gathering place. Mom and Dad surely pushed Dave and me in the stroller to Margaret Dean's home many times. She must've held us as infants and toddlers, but I don't recall her or these visits. I never asked Dave, who died in 1997, whether he had any memories of Great-grandma Dean. Dave was five when Margaret Dean died at age ninety in 1940. He may well have remembered her with his unusual power of early recall.

At any rate, Dave and I of the fifth generation overlapped the life of this ancient ancestor of the second generation. In our lifetimes, we physically touched relatives from the second to the seventh generations. We were able to do this because of the longevity of many of our ancestors. Several of my relatives lived to beyond ninety, and my mother to eighty-four.

Great-Grandfather Anthony Cawley ~ Endicott Pioneer

My net caught a few details about Great-grandfather Anthony Cawley. He left his blacksmith shop near Carbondale in Pennsylvania and moved with his family to Endicott. Mom saved his yellowing 1937 death notice. It read in part: "Mr. Cawley cast the first vote in the first village election here. He also mailed the first letter out of Endicott, and was the first treer in the Endicott-Johnson Corp., shoe factory, here." A treer did skillful finishing of upper leathers. He went from ancient blacksmithing to the industrial age in a single job move.

"My grandfather Anthony Cawley, your great-grandfather, eventually left the shoe factory and opened a cigar store downtown," Mom said. "He was gracious to his customers, always very refined. He was also a founding lay trustee of St. Ambrose Church in 1908."

Anthony Cawley and his family were pioneers. Endicott was incorporated as a village, in 1906, by a vote of forty-four to three. I wondered if other relatives, beyond Anthony, voted in the election. In a history of Endicott, I noted an early picture of Washington Avenue, the unpaved main street. It looked to me like a set from a John Ford western movie, and I easily imagined a gunfight there. A later photo suggested a quaint street with trees, like one painted by Norman Rockwell. In my day, parking meters replaced the trees and some of the charm was lost.

Great-Grandfather Thomas McDermott ~ Boisterous Boaster

Now a look at Dad's side of the family. "'I'm Thomas McDermott from near Pottsville in Schuylkill County, Pennsylvania,' he always boasted to one and all," my father said about his grandfather. "He was full of bluster and braggadocio." Dave and I pressed for more details.

"My grandfather wore a skimmer straw hat in summer and carried a black hawthorn walking stick," Dad added. "We were glad to see him on his visits to my mother." Dad's maternal grandfather, Thomas, was his favorite grandparent, and I presumed that he brought some warmth and humor into my father's bleak childhood in a coal mining family.

"I look forward to seeing my Grandfather Thomas McDermott in heaven. He was from near Pottsville," Dad said to me, decades later, while talking in a morphine haze and near death. I wished he had shared additional details about Thomas McDermott, but time ran out. I've thought about Dad's deathbed remark from time to time, and it always made perfect sense to me. Dad believed that heaven was more than an individualistic reward. Eternal life also included transformation of families and social groups into the death and resurrection of Jesus. His firm Christian hope prompted him to look forward to seeing his relatives again. I share that hope.

Whenever Joyce and I have driven by Pottsville, I responded to the mystique of the place by telling her that Great-grandfather McDermott boasted about his roots there.

"Pottsville was once a rough mining town with saloons, brothels, Yuengling Brewery, and even Molly Maguires skulking in the shadows. Yuengling Brewery is still making beer in Pottsville," I told Joyce. "John O'Hara, the novelist, also came from Pottsville, and literary critics have indicated that O'Hara wasn't boastful of his Pottsville origins. But Dad stressed that Thomas McDermott always bragged about Pottsville."

One night years ago, Joyce and I drove along I-81 in Pennsylvania. It was clear that with the snowy roads, we couldn't reach home in upstate New York. We decided to find lodging at the next exit, which by chance was the one for Pottsville. We found a motel and soon heard the car and truck traffic roaring by our close-to-the-road window. We were tired at breakfast after fitful sleep, but I still tried to romanticize the Pottsville area as the home of boisterous Tom.

"Well, it's not too impressive," Joyce observed, pointing to the downtown scene from the diner window. She was right. A new mall sat a mile away next to the interstate ramps, but downtown Pottsville was hurting. Friend Marti, who has connections to the paint store owner there, reported that Pottsville has since rebounded by the efforts of many citizens and business owners.

"Was Thomas a coal miner, brewery worker, politician, Molly Maguire?" I said to Joyce, as we drove north on I-81. "Why such a boaster about his locale? I wish I had met that colorful guy."

"You'll never know his full story," Joyce said.

"Unresolved loose ends are a challenge for generational storytellers. I often feel frustrated about thin data on the early generations."

I decided to indicate four traditions of our family early in this book. I presumed these traditions, in early generations, were firm and clear. Our family probably said in a collective, proud boast, "We're Irish-Americans. We're Catholics. We're Democrats. We're also Northerners. And we're ready to take on any objectors." Dissent in our early family was probably unthinkable, and few would have broken ranks. But life has a way of eventually challenging rigid traditions of ethnic families, especially in the melting pot of America. Some changes developed by my parents' fourth generation, and I witnessed many changes in the fifth through seventh generations.

We're Irish-Americans

I imagined that our early ancestors, as Irish-Americans, loved songs, stories, and traditions of Ireland and that St. Patrick's Day was their rite of spring. They must've bitterly resented employers with signs reading: "No Irish Need Apply." They stuck together for protection and support, and like other ethnic immigrants, married mostly within their culture. Dad of the fourth generation was probably the last of our family to tout himself as Irish. One day I heard him tell my classmate, "We're an Irish family." I later made a correction for my friend, "We're American with Irish background."

Public and later parochial schools blended ethnic immigrants, and in time, integrated those of different races. Dave and I of the fifth generation, influenced by the bubbling melting pot of public high school, made friends with Italian, Slovak, Greek, Jewish, Polish, Russian, Mexican, and other ethnic backgrounds; we didn't flaunt our Irish origins. We stressed the American rather than the Irish side of the coin. We began to understand the positive and negative features of Ireland and Irish-Americans as well as the strengths and weaknesses of other ethnic and racial groups. I'll later openly, boldly, and bravely risk confessing some negatives of the Irish and Irish-Americans.

We're Catholics

Our ancestors, and also Dave and I, were raised in the "Immigrant Catholic Church," a term applied to a church of mostly European immigrants in macro-America and also micro-parishes until the early 1960s. After the death of my mother in 1990, I found a large book in the attic called *The Catholic Faith*. It was more than one hundred years old and presented Catholic Christianity in clear and simple ways. I'm sorry now that I discarded that relic of the immigrant church. A similar book today would be, happily for me, more nuanced, complex, and flexible.

Local parishes gave immigrant Catholics strong religious support and traditional forms of Latin worship services. Early on, parishes were separated by geographical boundaries. St. Ambrose Church, and later Our Lady of Good Counsel Church, had territorial boundaries in Endicott. For decades our family had genuine affection for St. Ambrose parish and reluctantly joined Our Lady of Good Counsel Church when we moved to West Endicott. It was a traumatic change.

The Irish came to America already speaking English. As more and more immigrants arrived from Europe, they wanted priests who spoke their language. National parishes were created based on language, and these had no territorial boundaries. Italian, Polish, Slovak, and Eastern rite Catholic Churches were established in Endicott to serve corresponding ethnic families. As time went on, some ethnic families, through assimilation or the melting pot, chose to join the nearest Catholic Church. But some national parishes retained the membership of many parishioners, even when they had moved away from the ethnic neighborhood and parish to the suburbs.

By 2000, many liberal, moderate, and conservative Catholics had chosen to belong to parishes closest to their religious consciousness. Contemporary Catholics, searching for the right spiritual diet, claimed a parish that nourished their souls, even if this meant a longer drive on Sunday. What changes! First, territorial churches with lines, then supplemental national parishes without territorial lines, and now, for some Catholics, ideological churches.

"My own parish is packed each Sunday with a great many people who would flunk the punch test of official church thinking," Tim Unsworth of the *National Catholic Reporter* wrote, describing with humor his preferred liberal parish in the Chicago area. "Alcoholics Anonymous groups meet there every night; gays and lesbians pray with the entire community. Sinners must be very creative, because the liturgies are among the best in town. And the pastoral staff has ears the size of cab doors. Little wonder the place is called 'Our Lady of Thin Ice.'"

The European immigrant model of church in America, which extended roughly from the 1845 Irish Famine to the Second Vatican Council (1962-65), had strengths and weaknesses. (A second phase of the immigrant church has been developing more recently with many Hispanic, Asian, and other Catholic immigrants). On the positive side, the parish church and rectory, together with the parochial school and convent, formed a formidable fortress in a neighborhood. These immigrant parishes provided many services to their people.

Immigrant Catholics loved parishes that met their religious needs through worship services, their ethnic and social service needs in adjusting to America, and their educational needs. Praise and thanks were due to the immigrant families, dedicated sisters, and priests who together built effective local churches in America. A few immigrant pastors were rough-cut and lovable (or unlovable) tyrants, but the people tended to laugh at despots because priests championed their people. Parish loyalty was palpable, and competition with other parishes was inevitable.

This competition was clear in the Catholic Youth Organization's basketball games. Italians of St. Anthony's Church and Irish and others from St. Ambrose fought for bragging rights in Endicott; Poles of St. Stanislaus Kosta's Church and Slovaks from St. Ann struggled in Binghamton. Games were played in stuffy church halls or small parochial school gyms, and parents were part of the cheering sections. For decades the CYO League featured strong players, and local newspapers gave good ink to its games. Dave and I, as we'll see, played in many of those cataclysmic CYO games where luckily there were paid referees. The CYO facilitated the sublimation of ethnic rivalries into strongly contested basketball games so that street fights among Catholic youths of different ethnicities were kept to a reasonable and tolerable minimum.

On the negative side, the immigrant model of church was defensive, closed, and legalistic. The Second Vatican Council encouraged Catholics to lower their defenses and to be open to other Christians, Jews, and those from non-Biblical religions. Diamond-in-the-rough pastors were gone, and the people were increasingly college-educated, first at Catholic colleges and universities and then also at secular schools. Garrison Keillor, similar to Tim Unsworth, playfully called a Catholic parish "Our Lady of Perpetual Responsibility" to imply legalism. Moral theology gradually became more flexible and less legalistic before the council and continued this healthy trend afterwards.

In my view, Vatican Council II was the central religious event for Catholics in the twentieth century, and its sixteen official documents gave a freer vision and more flexible framework for church reform and renewal. Like most Catholics, our family members adapted to council changes, but some conservative Catholics, in clergy and laity, found changes to be a betrayal of the good old days. But I've held that those good old days, because of the negatives of the immigrant church, were not as good in reality as they seemed to some in the spirit of nostalgia.

We're Democrats

As Democrats, our early ancestors were probably unchangeable. I recalled that Grandpa Joe Cawley of the third generation had a framed picture of President Franklin D. Roosevelt and pasted on it the caption: "The Old Man." FDR was a father figure for many during the Depression and World War II, and Joe proudly hung President Roosevelt's picture in the office of his plumbing shop. Dad often stressed to Dave and me that the Democrats were for the workers. I recalled that Mom and Dad were glued to the TV for the Democratic National Conventions, but were detached toward the Republican Conventions and watched fewer hours.

After the presidential election of 1944 when I was eight, I learned that our family did not tolerate political heresy, specifically voting for Republicans.

"Don't ask Aunt Jule how she voted," Mom said to Dave and me. "She voted for Republican Wendell Willkie rather than Roosevelt four years ago. We don't want another family row if she voted for Dewey this time."

I never found out whether she voted for Republican Tom Dewey or not in 1944. In time I admired Aunt Jule, the family storyteller-seanachie prior to me, for her brave approach to freedom in voting, despite conscious and unconscious family assumptions and pressures to vote for Democrats on the local and national scenes.

We're Northerners

As Northerners, my ancestors were loyal to more than the Union Army. Irish immigrants tended to settle in urban areas and showed civic allegiance to cities in the northeast, such as Boston, New York, and Philadelphia. They also put down roots in cities along the Erie Canal in upstate New York (Albany, Utica, Syracuse, and Rochester), and in the port cities of the Great Lakes, such as Buffalo, Cleveland, and Chicago. The Chenango Canal and two railroads made the urban area of Binghamton attractive to Irish immigrants. Historians note that the Irish, by their numbers, took over urban police departments, fire departments, political machines, and the Catholic hierarchy. In my opinion, the Irish brought their strengths and weaknesses to these institutions. Some other ethnic immigrants put down roots on farms. Irish immigrant farmers were the exception to the urban rule.

"During the Depression, Grandpa Cawley and pal Sawyer found plumbing and construction jobs in Miami Beach, Florida, on Collins Avenue," my Mother told us. "He sent most of his pay to his family in Endicott and lived on the rest. Papa was homesick and came back with dark skin from outside work. I cried when we welcomed him home and heard his story of loneliness." It was unthinkable for Joe to move his family from the north to Florida even for work in the Depression.

Our family further claimed to be upstate New York Northerners. We lived 200 miles from New York City. I never learned where upstate New York exactly began. Some claimed it started at the Rip Van Winkle Bridge over the Hudson River; others drew lines north and west of the Catskill Mountains. A few jokers indicated that upstate began at the George Washington Bridge in view of New York City. Wherever the lines were drawn, our family and other upstaters were political and cultural rivals with the urban, and to us frantic, downstaters – especially those in "The City" (as we called New York City) or on Long Island.

Imperfection Works for Me

I've always considered our family of the four traditions to be ordinary and have adjusted to sins and imperfections in our Catholic Church, our family, and in myself. Dave and I had a running joke that genealogy was a dicey search that was bound to turn up, sooner or later, some blackguards and knaves. I sent him a gag card from Ireland and fudged that I saw several police-wanted posters with surnames very close to ours.

"Be careful what you wish for in genealogy," Dave said to me on my return home.

Like most Americans, our family came from the wrong side of the tracks in the early generations. The classic experience of immigrant families was for parents to work hard so that their children could have a better life through education. The status of families increased with each generation, and immigrant families were able to advance at work and in society, which allowed them to move across the tracks. Our family, in all its branches, followed this pattern.

Even though I've favored liberal politics, I occasionally quote conservative Whittaker Chambers from his masterfully crafted book *Witness*: "For, in America, most of us begin on the wrong side of the railroad tracks. The meaning of America, what made it the wonder of history and the hope of mankind, was that we were free not to stay on the wrong side of the railroad tracks. If within us there was something that empowered us to grow, we were free to grow and go where we could. Only, we were not free ever to forget, ever to despise our origins. They were our roots. They made us a nation."

I've guessed that no family member in our early generations had the internal need for any counseling from the family matriarch or male elder or general practitioner or parish priest to discover their identity. They knew exactly who they were – Irish-American, Catholic, Democratic Northerners, and I imagined they would've started a donnybrook if challenged seriously on any point. When I re-examined the four traditions in a later chapter, I found them more flexibly held.

It seems that Irish pride is what draws many to the Irish. The Irish don't need to "find themselves;" they already know who they are and they aren't afraid to display it. This flamboyant pride in their identity attracts others to share it with them. Perhaps the reason people of other ethnic groups enjoy Irish celebrations arises from the fierce pride of the Irish in their cultural heritage, and their special communion with spirits both worldly and unworldly. In brief, many have a touch of Irish in them, especially when it comes to Saint Patrick's Day.

In the next generation, I'll formally introduce my four grandparents. They all converged in Endicott, New York, with optimistic expectations in the early twentieth century.

"In the bottom of a large box of photos, I recently found
a picture of young Dave with the long Civil war rifle over his
shoulder." Aunt Jule with Jim and Dave, 1944.

"I only have a picture of Ellen McKeon McDermott."
She is seated second from left with her six daughters.
Extroverted husband Thomas McDermott and four sons
were not included in picture, c. 1900.

A. J. Cawley, Who Cast First Vote at Village Polls, Dies

A. J. Cawley, 90 years old, pioneer settler of Endicott, died at his home, 10 Madison Ave., this morning after a long illness.

Mr. Cawley cast the first vote in the first village election here. He also mailed the first letter out of Endicott, and was the first treer in the Endicott-Johnson Corp., shoe factory, here. He was a native of Carbondale, Pa., coming to Endicott shortly after its development began.

He is survived by one daughter, Mrs. H. J. Hanley; three sons, John, Joseph and Leo Cawley, all of Endicott; and one sister, Mrs. Ida Winthrope, California.

The body was removed to the Walter J. McCormack Funeral home, 605 E. Main St., where the funeral will be held Thursday morning at 9 o'clock, and at St. Ambrose church at 9:30. Rev. Alexis Hopkins, pastor, will officiate.

"Mom saved [Great-grandfather Anthony Cawley's] yellowing 1937 death notice."

"For decades our family had genuine affection for St. Ambrose parish…" Sturdy, black, functional railings were made by Grandfather Joe Cawley, master plumber, whose work was legendary for permanence, 1933.

Chapter Three

Third Generation: Optimistic Generation, 1880

"When I hear an Irish fiddle I think of the miners and the railroad workers and the immigrant Irish who had little else but brought their music with them. When I hear an Irish fiddle I know I have a soul."

Patricia Harty, "A Darker Shade of Green" in
Being Irish

Third Generation: Four Grandparents

Paternal Side   Maternal Side

Paternal Side	Maternal Side
J. J. Cuddy	Joseph Cawley
Julia McDermott	Harriet Dean
Seven children	Five children

Two of our four grandparents, according to records, were born in the 1880s, and I presume the other two were in the same age range. Dave and I knew three grandparents well and one only in passing. As teens, our grandparents accompanied their parents into the twentieth century. Family hopes centered on Endicott, New York where the new Endicott-Johnson shoe factories were like magnets drawing immigrants of different ethnic backgrounds.

"We had sold the Dean farm and moved to Endicott," Grandma Harriet Dean Cawley said to me. "Watching horses drawing wagon-loads of dirt from the big pits during the building of the foundations for the E-J shoe factories was exciting. We were optimistic about the future."

George F. ~ Benevolent Father of Endicott

After George F. Johnson expanded shoe manufacturing from nearby Johnson City to Endicott, a new and unusual village grew under his paternalistic guidance. George F., as everyone called him, was committed to the welfare of the workers as well as to profits. He provided houses at very low interest, and many sections in Endicott were developed by E-J for its workers. Grandpa Cuddy, an E-J worker, wisely purchased one. E-J gave free family health care with a team of doctors, an amazing benefit.

George F. funded parks with swimming pools for his workers and other residents of the community. He purchased six carousels, which are still functional and enjoyed by the current generation of children in the Triple Cities of Endicott, Johnson City, and Binghamton. He insisted that the carousels be free of charge. That policy continues, but local governments now run them.

The E-J Band provided concerts in the parks, and the annual B.C. Open Golf Tournament under the Professional Golf Association is now held at En-Joie facilities in Endicott, formerly an E-J golf course. George F. donated expensive pipe organs to local churches, including St. Ambrose Church. Anyone could eat with the workers in the E-J cafeteria, and Dave and I, along with high school friends, sometimes ate there next to the workers, for a pittance.

The annual Labor Day celebration, funded by E-J, was a vast community event. Residents of the Triple Cities flocked to the grandstand behind Union-Endicott High School for the all-day celebration, which included high-wire acts and vaudeville entertainment. The prize of $20.00, a great sum in those days, was taped to the top of a greased pole, and several older boys took turns trying to climb to the money. An hour usually elapsed before the winner grabbed the money and slid down in ruined clothes to applause. If my memory is accurate, a guy named Mulligan won for several years.

"I want to enter the greased pole contest," Dave, at age twelve, declared.

"You'll stain your clothes, and I'll end up trying to wash them," Mom said, holding firm.

"Well, I'm going to enter the pie eating contest." He won $5.00 for first place by eating a whole pie with his hands behind his back in the quickest time, and Mom washed the huckleberry stains from his shirt on the next washday.

The grand finale was an hour-long fireworks display. We never missed the massive and colorful fireworks. As a teen, I imagined the exploding thunder rolling up the Susquehanna River valley toward Binghamton and down the valley toward Owego. Pyrotechnics later in life, even those by Disney World, always seemed by comparison anemic. My mind always went back to the overwhelming and magical experience of Labor Day fireworks in Endicott.

Joe Cawley ~ Accessible Grandfather

My grandfather, Joe Cawley, son of Anthony Cawley and Julia Coggins, was a prominent man in my life, and I have many stories about him. In our discussions throughout the years, Dave and I sometimes made him into a man of mythic proportions. In fact, on one level he was an ordinary and humorous man with strengths and weaknesses, but he had noteworthy gifts as well.

"When Papa held you as toddlers he liked to give back-rubs," Mom told us. "He was affectionate, but vigorous." He was also an accessible grandfather to his eight grandchildren. "You can call me Joe," he said to us until we complied.

I remembered one time Joe was driving his plumbing truck with Dave and me in the other seat. He had an ivory skeleton's head mounted on the shifting stick, and his pipes and tools were bouncing and clanging. It was great fun. The ride and the skeleton's head were near the cellar floor of my memory. Dave was six, I guessed, and I was five.

Because we lived in a duplex only two blocks from Joe's home, Dave and I regularly stopped by there on errands for Mom. Once I carried a bowl of pumpkin filling which overflowed onto my shirt and pants. Joe cleaned me up and told me not to worry about minor things. Sometimes we popped in for the fun of it and played in his office with his hand-crank adding machine. He smoked regularly and saved tinfoil wrappings to enlarge the tin ball on his desk. It eventually became a heavy ball, like those shot-putters use, and Dave and I checked it out on nearly every visit.

Joe was a hardworking plumber, and his son Andrew was his partner. On the sides of their trucks were bold letters: **Cawley & Son Plumbing and Heating**. When he returned home at night after his house calls, Joe was as black as a coal miner. He had his own washroom in the cellar where he cleaned up for supper. Dave and I sometimes watched as he tried to clean grime from his hands, arms, and face with Babbo cleanser and gritty Lava soap.

Joe called Mom, one summer vacation day, and suggested that Dave and I, about nine and eight, go plumbing with him again. As usual, we dropped everything and ran to his home-based business two blocks away. At the first house call, Dave brought in several tools as needed.

"Seamus, I need the big wrench behind the driver's seat," Joe said to me in the cellar of the second house. I didn't understand why he called me that and thought it was just a pet name. Only later did I discover that Seamus was Gaelic for James. As he drove from stop to stop, he talked to us as equals about World War II and his favorite baseball team, the New York Yankees. Joe kidded and teased us, and when he spontaneously sang several bars of "Galway Bay," Dave and I hummed along. Joe sometimes called us scamps (rascals) as a term of endearment.

We usually went straight home after a work outing, but on this humid day we stopped at a workers' saloon. Joe seated us at a quiet table and provided soda and pretzels. He had a beer and chatted briefly with others. The door suddenly flew open, and in strode a desperado with rubber boots to the knee and with two roughnecks in tow. The leader made a dramatic spit toward the brass spittoon without even losing stride and missed. The trio sat at a table in the rear.

"Maybe there'll be a gunfight," I whispered excitedly to Dave. By then we had seen many cowboy films.

"Nobody has guns in here," he said, showing the superiority of an older brother.

"Then maybe there'll be a fight with chairs broken over their heads," I said, pointing to the bad guys. Joe soon gave a signal that it was time to go. I was disappointed that nothing exciting had happened beyond the errant spitting.

"Joe, are those three guys in boots outlaws?" I asked in the truck.

"No, they're harmless, hard workers from the tannery in their rubber boots. You should respect working folks." Dave chuckled, but didn't say, "I told you so."

When Joe dropped us off at our home at 43 Jackson Avenue, he followed his generous ritual. He reached in the pocket of his blue bib-overalls and pulled out a fistful of coins and a few loose dollar bills. Without counting, he gave it all to Dave.

"You split this up and don't tell your mother I paid you." We thanked him and waited for his usual parting advice. "So long, Dave. Keep your nose clean," he said. "Seamus, the same."

"So long, Joe," we yelled as he drove off. Dave pocketed the cash for dividing later.

As we grew older and stronger, we became more helpful to Joe. I remembered another plumbing day when Joe was about sixty-four years old, Dave fourteen, and I thirteen. We drove to a street lined with older houses. Joe had to cut a hole through a cellar wall to run a pipe. He kept a long tool, like a spear, for such breakthroughs in his truck. Joe carefully measured three times and scratched an X on the wall.

"Always measure several times," he told us, sharing some of his working wisdom. He grasped the spear toward the point, Dave held the middle, and I grabbed the far end. "Boys, start on three," he said. "One, two, THREE."

Thud, thud, thud. Each thrust of the spear sent vibrations along the tool, down my arms, down my spinal cord, and down my legs to my rattling toes. Thud, thud, thud. Again thud, thud, thud, and then breakthrough. It was a sweltering day, and the cellar was covered with dust and cobwebs. When we got home, Mom said Dave and I looked like raccoons because of the dust and grime around our eyes. Dad said we resembled Pennsylvania coal miners at the end of a shift. I prized that day because I learned the value of honest physical labor from a dedicated workman. Mom and Dad were pleased because we learned the family tradition of hard work.

"Joe was a man of humor, but he also had an Irish temper. Sometimes he exploded," Dad said. "One time when he couldn't find any wooden matches in his truck or office or home, he bought 144 large boxes of stick matches. He hoped never to run out of matches again."

Joe had a habit of striking his stick matches against the thigh of his trousers. Dave and I liked to watch Joe's match go "whoosh" as it ignited. He held it high for two seconds, like the Statue of Liberty holds her torch. He later carefully flicked his ashes into the cuffs of his pants if an ashtray was not immediately available, and small burn holes sometimes scarred his cuffs.

Mom's favorite story about Joe involved a rocking chair. She told it many times without any variation in details. "Papa was rocking in a just-purchased secondhand chair and reading his newspaper. He suddenly rocked over backward, and Andrew, my sisters, and I tried to stifle our giggles. He put it right side up, and again he solemnly rocked and read, but then over he went again.

"'Open the front door!' he shouted as he angrily scrambled to his feet.

"'Oh no, Papa!' we pleaded. 'Think of the neighbors.'

"'I don't care about the neighbors! Open the door!' he repeated.

"Andrew was happy to open the door, and Papa threw the rocking chair into the front yard. We ran out the back door and didn't come back inside until we had finally stopped laughing," Mom finished her story, smiling at the memory.

Blackberry season was a favorite time for Joe. When Dave and I were about fifteen and fourteen, he organized a family outing for blackberry picking. In two cars, the family drove toward the Pennsylvania border and took a side road to the top of the hill. We stopped at the farm that the Deans once owned and called "Mount Joy." Joe went inside and asked permission of the current owner for us to pick berries along one of his fields.

Joe then led us to a spot that he had found productive in prior Augusts. The branches were sagging with ripe berries, and Dave and I did more eating than picking. Others filled pots and kettles with plump blackberries. Back home Grandma Cawley made pie shells and waited for our return. This story was one of the last to be retrieved from the files of my memory for this chapter. It all came back to me when I read the poem, "Blackberry Picking," by Seamus Heaney, the Nobel Prize-winning Irish poet:

> You ate that first one and its flesh was sweet
> Like thickened wine: summer's blood was in it
> Leaving stains upon the tongue and lust for
> Picking . . .

When I was about twenty and a seminary student – inexperienced seminarians can be a self-righteous lot – some family members asked me to stop by and visit with Joe. I was asked to remind him gently of the opportunities for Confession and Holy Communion. Some older Catholics were committed to Sunday Mass, but had a custom of using these sacraments less frequently. I really should've known better. He smiled, and I realized that he knew this was a setup. He gave me a Bible lesson: "Seamus, I've always liked the gospel story, told by Jesus, how one man prayed with great boasting, but the tax collector only prayed, 'Oh God, be merciful to me a sinner.'"

Joe implied that we were like the boaster and he was like the contrite taxman. I quickly changed the subject to cover my embarrassment. Others later asked me how it went. "Joe knows more about the meaning of the Christian faith than we do," I said. "We can learn from him."

Dave was with Joe when he died at age seventy-one. Although he had been in and out of the hospital a few times, he wanted to be at home. Joe was in his extra sturdy rocking chair and suddenly stopped breathing. Dave called Monsignor Sheehan for the last rites. At his wake, many grateful strangers came to pay their respects. Because Joe worked in many homes, he knew the poverty of some families during the Depression years and quietly sent food boxes to help. Recipients of his generosity came to his wake. Others told how he carried plumbing bills without charging any interest for years during hard times. Joe Cawley may not have been a famous man, but he was a good and generous man. His eight grandchildren knew that from their earliest years.

Grandma Harriet Dean Cawley ~ Strong and Admirable Woman

Grandmother Harriet Dean Cawley, daughter of James Dean and Margaret Hartigan, was called *Doll* because of her striking looks. She was well known and well liked in Endicott. As she grew older, she became respected for her formidable style.

Few dared to challenge or cross her, but she was a softy toward her grandchildren.

"I've a freshly baked pie at home. Send one of the boys to pick it up," Grandma sometimes said to Mom after Sunday mass. Mom would dispatch Dave or me to race over to get it. Blackberry pie was Gram's specialty, but she would switch to apple pie, with a longer season for apples. I didn't care about the kind of pie; they were all delicious, except for her mincemeat pie.

Grandma Cawley was James Joycean in her stream-of-consciousness style of visiting. She often went from one witty story to another with a quick breath. In my middle age, I sometimes stopped by to visit her. It was not really a dialogue, but I learned many family stories about her side. Once I nodded off to sleep during one of her stories. She nudged me and said, "These family stories are worth remembering." I later interpreted "worth remembering" to mean that I should hear her family tales and pass them on.

"In the 1920s, the Ku Klux Klan marched in white robes and hoods in Endicott to protest too many Catholics and foreigners," Grandma Cawley began an oft-told story. "As the marchers passed the fire station downtown, an alarm sounded to summon the fire trucks to a site several blocks away. The trucks broke up the parade to the joy of most citizens, myself included." I imagined the Klan's spoiled parade and the laughter and hooting of my grandmother and other citizens along Washington Avenue. "And that false alarm was a fortunate coincidence," she said, looking like the feline that swallowed the goldfinch.

"That was no coincidence. What really happened?" I asked, surprising myself by this challenge.

"Well, it was a planned false alarm, and I know the boy who pulled the alarm," she whispered, as if police were bugging her home forty years after the event. "He was a good friend of my son Andrew." I was surprised that she didn't tell me the name of Andrew's friend. For reasons of timing, an accomplice must have phoned from the parade site to the alarm-puller blocks away to say that the KKK was at the fire station. I later guessed that the second boy might've been Andrew.

I've also concluded that Grandma was involved, or at least knew all of the false alarm conspirators, though she wouldn't tell me. I'll never know for sure whether my attractive, strong, refined, and witty Grandma Cawley would've been an indictable co-conspirator. I don't condone false alarms, but in view of the good purpose of opposing KKK bigotry against Catholics and foreigners (most of the foreigners were Catholics) I must make a rare exception. I've always felt that this one story caught the spirit of our family in the 1920s. My Irish-Catholic ancestors, scarred by memories of the Famine and hardened by years on the lower rungs of the economic ladder, weren't going to be intimidated by cowardly KKK marchers in white robes and hoods. I've often wished that Dave and I were alive in those days and could've been in on the action.

Grandma also told me about the annual collection of food from Irish and other ethnic farmers when she was still on the farm. "Two Sisters from St. Mary's Orphanage and a volunteer driver visited farm families and received donations of vegetables, live chickens, pies, honey, and butter. At harvest time they came in a Conestoga wagon pulled by a team of horses," she said. I thought she meant to say Canastota, an Erie Canal town about ninety miles away. While driving home, I wondered whether Grandma was losing her mental sharpness. Out of curiosity, I looked up the word in my dictionary and found that she was right. I'd never heard of a Conestoga wagon, but Grandma and *Webster* had.

In these visits with my grandmother, I noticed a constant theme of loneliness. It was as if Grandma were a student of Frank O'Connor, who wrote so well about human loneliness in many short stories. She often used the word *lonesome* in her conversations. "She was *lonesome* as a child, and needed to be rocked," Grandma said to me from her rocking chair about one of my seven cousins on the Cawley side of the family. "My neighbor Orie was a *lonesome* man," she said in a spirit of empathy in one of her stories.

"Grandma's own loneliness was due to her isolation from long years of deafness despite her early-model and late-model hearing aids," Mom said. That helped to explain her depression when her daughter Frances died at forty-four. The day after the funeral Grandma fled to her brother's home just over the line into Pennsylvania and remained there for months. She struggled toe-to-toe with grief and the mystery of premature death. Gram was a great pray-er, and, like Jacob, she wrestled with God in prayer. When she completed the acute stage of the process of grieving, she came home on her own terms. Lonesome or not, Grandma Harriet Dean Cawley was a strong and admirable woman.

Grandpa J. J. Cuddy ~ Little Known Grandfather

Grandpa J. J. Cuddy, born of John Cuddy and Catherine Tobin, began work early in life as a coal miner in Pennsylvania. He married Julia McDermott from near Pottsville in Schulykill County. J. J. – I never heard him called by any other name – moved his family to Endicott and became a tinsmith at E-J. In time he was legally separated from Grandma Cuddy. Dave and I saw him from time to time, but unfortunately we never had a relationship with him.

In old age, J. J. was spitting up black coal dust from his younger days in the coalmines. I remembered that our family talked several times about short-term dangers in coal mining and the long-term peril of black lung. When I visited him in his final year, he seemed to be a lonely figure. One drawback of being the designated storyteller is that some stories are fragmented. J. J. Cuddy remained for me an unsolved mystery.

Grandma Julia McDermott Cuddy ~ Earth Mother

I found it easy to write about Grandma Julia McDermott Cuddy, born of extroverted Thomas McDermott and Ellen McKeon. Grandma Cuddy was an earth mother to her seven children and many grandchildren. Warm, friendly, and uncomplicated, she naturally folded young Dave and me into her arms. I felt peaceful on her lap, and my memories about her are positive.

"A black sky foretold a coming storm. My mom ran and gathered up little chicks into her apron," Dad said, recalling a scene from his childhood. "Your Grandma was the mothering type."

We visited Grandma's home on foot in the early days and often enjoyed a lunch with several cousins on the Cuddy side of the family. She slathered big gobs of French's mustard on bologna sandwiches for us. Gram Cuddy was at her best with her seven sons and daughters or her large brood of chick-like grandchildren around her table.

The debate about the moral tone of bingo was a swamp that I've tried to avoid, but cannot. For decades some Catholic churches as well as nonprofit groups have been involved in this type of fundraising. I knew of one church that grossed $1 million and netted over $300,000 in ten years, but this form of gambling was offensive to some Catholics and many Protestants. I can only report the social enjoyment of Grandma Cuddy, who played bingo regularly. Coached by Dad, Dave and I often asked her, "How did you do at bingo, Grandma?" She always reported wins of $10.00 or $20.00 and occasional jackpots. We joked among ourselves about her reluctance to report losses. Through the years, I've noticed that gamblers of any stripe talk readily of their good luck, and are experts at concealing their bad fortune.

Grandma Cuddy lived on River Terrace along the east branch of the Susquehanna River, a long river winding from Cooperstown, New York to Chesapeake Bay. In spring the swollen river sometimes caused serious flood damage. Before rising water reached a dangerous level for us, Dave and I, like Huck Finn and Tom Sawyer, watched the annual floodwaters carry logs, tables, chairs, farm sheds, and once a coop with chickens trapped inside past Grandma's house. Sometimes Gram had water in her cellar.

"Like Noah, she stayed in her ark-home during a flood," Dad said. "We asked her a few times to evacuate to higher ground, but she never budged." Only after World War II did the Army Corps of Engineers finally build high levees to control the Susquehanna River during the flood season.

In the middle of Grandma's living room was a large circular heating grate built into the floor of her E-J home. This was the warmest place in the house, and five or six of us would be on or near the grate chatting and laughing. The women discreetly held down their dresses. Our family did not tolerate billowing dresses, like the one Marilyn Monroe later made famous. Although the heating grate was not a stone fireplace with aesthetic features, it was our hearth, and Dave and I were warm and comfortable there with Grandma Cuddy and others at our side.

The only time I saw a different side to cheerful Grandma was when she reminisced and mentioned that a family in Pennsylvania was Welsh. She made such a sour face when saying "Welsh" that I was surprised. I read later that the Welsh were often on the management side in the coal mining industry of northeast Pennsylvania. In labor struggles, the Irish and other ethnic miners saw them as oppressors. This explained Grandma's sour expression.

"I decided to throw out junk accumulated in the attic throughout the years," said Aunt Helen who lived with Grandma Cuddy. "I pitched worthless things out the attic window into the yard. When I went out to the yard to haul the sorry mess to the curb, I found only a few broken items. After searching the house, I found that Mom had neatly piled the discarded items, made worse by the fall from attic to yard, down in the cellar near the coal bin." This story became part of Grandma's Irish wake when we reminisced about the long life of Julia McDermott Cuddy.

After Grandma's funeral, Dad told about an Irish wake that he experienced as a youth in Pennsylvania. The grieving family served food, sweets, tea, beer, and provided a box of clay pipes for smokers. In telling and re-telling this story, the clay pipes always fascinated Dad. I recently read old stories about the harsh life in the Blasket Islands, now uninhabited, off the tip of Dingle Peninsula in County Kerry. A death on the big island prompted a boat to be dispatched to the mainland for a barrel of beer and a box of clay pipes, and the islanders provided food for the wake. Irish wakes are therapeutic as Martha Manning in *Chasing Grace* notes, "In death, as in life, we will be Irish – surrounded by our friends and family, by the music we love, by grand stories inflated with every telling, by drinking and eating (in that order), by the free flow of tears, and by one of the greatest comforts in grief: a couple of straight shots of laughter."

E-J & IBM ~ Positives and Negatives

Before moving on to the next generation, I want to share my brief evaluation of industrial relations in Endicott. I admit my bias for generally seeing the positives rather than the negatives of E-J and IBM in our mostly two-company village. On the bright side, E-J workers erected two dramatic stone arches across Main Street, one in Endicott and one in Johnson City. Each arch boasted: "Home of the Square Deal." Most E-J workers were generally satisfied, especially to have work in the Depression and to receive generous benefits. On the dark side, E-J wages were low, but at the same time IBM gave good benefits and higher pay. This wage difference was felt by E-J workers and subtly divided our village.

Some charged that E-J provided welfare capitalism or paternalistic socialism for its workers who received many unusual and generous benefits, but for the most part didn't have unions to safeguard their rights and improve wages. There were votes during the years about unions at E-J, but organizers never made significant inroads.

Another negative was the pungent smell of E-J tanneries. The fetid hides of cattle came by train from Omaha and Chicago meat packers. Remnants of flesh from the meat packing process still clung to the inside of the hides; the outside bristled with hair. Tannery workers slogged in boots as they pulled the hides from one chemical vat to another. On a windy day, the stench blew into some residential neighborhoods. Clogged sinuses opened up at once upon the first whiff of the foul odor. Tannery workers were well paid, but their work was smelly, strenuous, and wet. I recently heard stories about demanding tannery work from high school classmate, Fran Fetsko. During his college years, he worked summers in the tannery.

During the Depression, E-J faced stiff competition at home and abroad and began a long downward slide, despite some upturn during World War II. During subsequent decades, local shoe manufacturing shrank and phased out of Endicott. Many E-J factory buildings, rather than being left to rust and rot, were gradually torn down. As a native of Endicott, I've felt sad whenever I passed the former E-J area. The shoe industry, once so vibrant, was gone, and with it much of our past vanished.

IBM has also contributed to Endicott in remarkable ways. The industry began in Endicott in 1911 with the name of International Time Recording Company. Thomas J. Watson, Sr. took the reins in 1914; the name of International Business Machines dates back to 1924. IBM fulfilled the pot-of-gold hopes of its workers in Endicott.

Some criticized IBM for its white-shirt policy for male office workers. My father wore a white shirt every workday and Sunday. Others thought IBM's control over workers, its corny company songs, and obsessive work culture were excessive. Welfare capitalism again provided many generous benefits to workers, but without unions. The social justice teachings of the Catholic Church encouraged me to support unions, but Dave and I never debated the lack of unions at IBM and E-J.

Dad and Dave had long careers at IBM. From their positive experiences at IBM and my observations, I've concluded that IBM employees were pleased to have jobs with high wages and generous benefits in a growing and thriving company, despite any drawbacks. After decades of growth, even IBM downsized in Endicott and elsewhere in its vast world empire, in the '80s, '90s, and in the new millennium.

Golden Age or Tarnished Age?

I remember growing up toward the end of a Golden Age in Endicott, especially for young people. E-J provided many opportunities for recreation for all residents. The IBM Country Club was open to families of IBM workers, and Dave and I enjoyed golfing on its two courses, swimming, and bowling. The Boys Club was another center for us with its endless tournaments in pool, ping-pong, basketball, and tennis. Public and parochial schools provided many opportunities for sports and competition. I thought all young people in America had such comprehensive and free recreational opportunities. After I left Endicott in 1954, I learned how spoiled we were. Perhaps I've mythologized Endicott by my description of a Golden Age. No village can live up to such a claim. Of course it had a police department, a jail, and some dark sides. There were a few rough streets where even the resident junkyard dogs patrolled in packs.

Another dark element surfaced in the book of Endicott's local historian James E. Fiori. Anglo-Saxon and Irish buyers could purchase homes in some special areas of the south end of Endicott, but those with other European backgrounds were excluded due to deed restrictions. Newer immigrant families clustered on the northside. Housing discrimination and nativism were clearly part of Endicott's history. I have no illusion about the preferential treatment of the Irish in Endicott. If the Irish, my family included, had not arrived in America earlier and had not spoken English upon arrival, I'm sure that they too would have been discriminated against and excluded by deed restrictions.

Golden Age or Tarnished Age? I'm peaceful with Slightly Tarnished Age. As an adult, I've come to understand that imperfection characterizes individuals, families, workplace, politics, medicine, social services, church, and everything else. But I also remember many positives that I experienced growing up in Endicott. I didn't construe Endicott as a Camelot Village, but I always sensed that despite any negatives, a subtle magical atmosphere surrounded my native place.

My four grandparents had entered the twentieth century with high hopes. They gradually improved their lot and probably presumed that the pot-of-gold economy would continue indefinitely. In the next chapter, my parents will be formally introduced. John and Veronica Cuddy will face the Depression, which began in 1929 and lasted over a dozen years. They will be more realistic than their parents about pots-of-gold, the length of good times, and boomtowns.

"Lonesome or not, Grandma Harriet Dean Cawley
was a strong and admirable woman." 1905.

"Joe Cawley may not have been a famous man, but he was a
good and generous man. His eight grandchildren knew that…"
Joe Cawley with four grandchildren: from left to right, Jim and
Dave Cuddy, Joyce Hickey; Marie Hickey on his shoulder; Aunt
Frances Doyle in rear, 1940.

"Gram Cuddy was at her best with her seven sons and daughters
or her large brood of chick-like grandchildren around her table."
1904.

"Grandma Cuddy was an earth mother..."
Three generation photo: Dave (5th gen.), left, with infant Becky,
(6th gen.), and Grandma Cuddy, (3rd gen.), 1959.

Chapter Four

Fourth Generation: Depression Generation, 1906

"Despite the financial setbacks of the Depression years, the American Irish continued to climb the economic ladder, participating in the post-World War II prosperity that carried many to the suburbs and on to college and graduate school, with help from the G. I. Bill."

Ann Kathleen Bradley, History of the Irish in America

Fourth Generation: Two Parents

Father	Mother
John Cuddy	Veronica Cawley
Oldest of seven children	Oldest of five children

John Cuddy, son of J. J. Cuddy and Julia McDermott, was born on May 27, 1906, near Wilkes-Barre, Pennsylvania. Veronica Cawley, daughter of Joe Cawley and Harriet Dean, was born on September 3, 1906, in Endicott, New York. They met in front of St. Ambrose Church in Endicott, at age fourteen, and in time chose "Margie" for their song. They belonged to the Depression generation.

Hardships of the Depression

The Great Depression began in 1929 and ended by the mid-'40s. In my view of this generation, those with major scars from hard times squeezed the green ink out of their dollar bills until the day they died. A few survived with only scratches and became free and easy in their spending when good times reappeared. John and Veronica were in the middle with minor scars.

"My Model T Ford was in good shape except for one flaw," Dad said, in a spirit of wistful reminiscing to Dave and me. "It wouldn't go up a steep hill in any of the forward gears. Driving to Ithaca for a picnic we had no problems, but leaving town I had to back up a four-mile hill. I sold it to help fund our wedding. We couldn't afford a car during hard times."

They had wanted to marry sooner, but the Depression delayed them for four years. Mom was sensitive about marrying late in life, at twenty-seven. After the wedding at St. Ambrose Church, they rode the train to New York City for their honeymoon. Pictures of the family send-off at the train station showed them beaming with joy. After their return, John and Veronica continued to deal with the challenges of tough times. In the middle of the Depression, their lives changed considerably when they became parents of two sons.

"During the Depression, we left our stroller in front of Hamlin's Drugstore and were gone for a few minutes. Someone stole it," Mom told us, still amazed that anyone would do such a thing. "That's how bad things were, even in quiet Endicott." I was surprised at another of her memories: "We usually paid our Christmas bills by May." Dave and I were oblivious of hard times.

"The owner of a corner market allowed some families, ours included, to charge groceries during the Depression," Dad said, relating a bitter story. "Preferring to wait on cash customers first, he made me stand aside and wait one day. I was furious, and on the next payday, I paid him off and told him off. We never bought from him again." Dave and I were forbidden ever to go there. We didn't, even for penny candy, because family honor was at stake.

Some Depression stories were bittersweet. Our parents saved and bought snowsuits for Dave and me, navy blue wool coats and bib pants when we were seven and six. During Christmas vacation, a storm covered Endicott with snow, and Dave and I, clothed in our snowsuits, ventured out with sleds to enjoy the day. We discovered some empty cardboard boxes behind the A&P market and found it was more fun using the boxes to slide down the hill, rather than our sleds. In time the boxes disintegrated, so we decided to slide without cardboards or sleds. Large holes eventually opened on all four knees of our snow pants.

"We're in big trouble. Maybe we should run away," Dave suggested, grasping for straws. "No, I've got a better idea. We'll slip in the backdoor and hang these up as soon as we can."

I respected his know-how and extra year of experience and agreed. It sounded better than running away in winter. If we had run away, we probably wouldn't have gone any farther than two blocks to Joe Cawley's warm cellar.

We tried to sneak into the house, but Dad intercepted us. He saw the damage immediately, spanked us, and sent us to bed early. We found no ally in Mom; she, too, was steaming. She neatly patched our pants, and we knew better than to complain. We could not laugh about this story until after the Depression.

Our family lived in a rented duplex at 43 Jackson Avenue within walking distance of IBM. Three bedrooms allowed Dave and me to have our own rooms. A truck delivered two kinds of coal, chestnut hard coal for the furnace and tiny pea coal for the hot water heater. The whole house shook when a trucker dispatched two tons of coal down a chute and through a cellar window into the coal bin. Because the A&P market's back door was nearby, Dad instructed Dave and me to rummage through the discards and to bring home orange crates for kindling wood for both furnace and water heater. We felt no shame in this chore.

The Depression prompted inventive ways for young and old to make money. The best story of moxie during the bad times came to me not from a member of our family, but from Frank Gaube of Binghamton. I shared this story with Dad, and he re-told it to others.

"I got up early and delivered the morning papers with my wagon," Frank started, with a far-off look in his eyes. "I always ordered an extra paper for the men at the bakery and gave it to them without charge for six free donuts. I ate one and gave five donuts to the men at the maintenance shop of the Delaware, Lackawanna, and Western Railroad. For the donuts they gave me two large chunks of ice, which I put in the wagon and delivered to nearby families for a few pennies a week. After cocoa and oatmeal at home, I walked to St. Paul's School. I must have been in the eighth grade." I wasn't surprised that Frank later became an executive at Ansco Film in Binghamton.

Though money and supplies were tight, the following scene happened several times at our home before and during the war years. Dave and I, upon answering the doorbell, encountered a raggedy man pleading for food.

"Wait here and I'll get Mom," Dave said.

"Mom, there's another tramp asking for food."

"Invite him to come to the back porch." Mom made a big sandwich and found an orange soda in the refrigerator and served him a paper napkin with his lunch. She chatted with him for a while. In retrospect, I've thought that if Mom had been out of paper napkins, she would've given him a cloth napkin. Dave and I went out and tried to make small talk with our guest. Movie critic Pauline Kael told about her mother giving food to those in need from the back porch during the Depression. Some fearful neighbors asked when she would stop feeding the poor. Her mother said she would feed them till the food ran out. Mom Cuddy was like that. No matter how little we had, she knew others had less and accommodated them when she could.

The Depression ended at different times for families on Jackson Avenue. I recalled when it ended for us. Pay went up during WWII, and lots of overtime-fattened paychecks. Like a professional forger, Mom always endorsed Dad's paycheck before she went to the A&P market to cash it and shop. Dave and I admired how coolly she signed Dad's signature, always after one practice try on scrap paper.

"Dad often makes over $100.00 a week with war overtime," she said to Dave and me. "The Depression is finally over for us," she added, with tears in her eyes. Looking back, I believe it was 1944.

John Cuddy ~ Horatio Alger Type

As the oldest of seven children, my father John Cuddy had too many responsibilities at too early an age. His childhood stories were not happy. John and his six brothers and sisters, in Pennsylvania, had to pick up coal along the railroad tracks for use at home. He told us stories of running to the corner tavern with a tin pail, called a growler, for draft beer for the neighbors. An occasional tip of a penny brightened his day.

The poverty of the Cuddys gave way to gradual improvement after moving to Endicott. John's story was straight out of Horatio Alger books. He boasted that he read those books that showed how hard work and hustle paid off. By high school, John looked like singer Bing Crosby, and many kidded him about the resemblance. He took business courses at Union-Endicott High School, graduated, and began a series of steps up the economic ladder.

An excellent typist, John worked in offices of the Delaware, Lackawanna, and Western Railroad and *The Binghamton Press*. At age twenty-nine, he luckily secured a job at IBM in the pit of the Depression. In his thirty-three-year career at IBM, he gradually refined his role of Administrative Associate. At one point, John became "AAAGM-IBM-E," Administrative Associate to the Assistant General Manager of IBM-Endicott. As a high school graduate, he enjoyed the role of ghostwriter for college grads. Dad shared with us that his reports and speeches required few, if any, changes by his bosses.

I recalled that Dad bought a used IBM electric typewriter for home use. When typing, he attacked the machine with intensity and precision.

"You'll set that typewriter on fire if you don't let it cool down," I said, watching him type a long personal letter one day.

"You should've seen me as a young typist. I was really fast then."

During the war Dad was manager of an office of thirty women. I remembered him talking with Mom about occasional employee problems. I learned that at first he tried to please each worker. "Dad gradually learned from experience how to manage people in a more realistic way," Mom explained to Dave and me years later. Dave, with the management gene from Dad, spent thirty-eight years with IBM and rose to several key management positions. I must have inherited Dad's writing gene.

Dad was a strong Catholic, but he also developed mature flexibility in his conscience. Dave and I were Cub Scouts with meetings in the basement of the nearby Methodist Church. On Scout Sunday, scouts of all faiths were invited to attend Methodist services in a group. Such a question was resolved long ago – Catholics should not attend such services.

"You boys can go," Dad consented. "As parent, I'll take full responsibility for this decision." A few years later, Dave and I wanted to join the YMCA in Binghamton to use the indoor pool. Others had decided that issue already – not allowed because of the Y's historical connection with the Protestant faith. Again as parent, he chose flexibility. At the YMCA, Dave and I enjoyed many swims, and no lifeguard or swimmer raised any religious issues.

Veronica Cawley ~ Wake, Ladder, Listening

Veronica Cawley, the first of five children, enjoyed an easier early life than did John. As the firstborn, she received considerable attention. We have many photos of Veronica growing up and wearing attractive outfits. Dave saw her as a princess in her family.

"Looking back, I took a lot for granted," Mom told Dave and me. "Papa put his plumbing aside and tried running a restaurant for two years. I would openly help myself to coins from the cash register, and he never scolded me for this."

One of my earliest memories of Mom, when I was six, involved Tim Haggerty's Irish wake held at his home. We traveled by afternoon bus to Binghamton to pay our respects and offer sympathy. She carried one of her famous chocolate cakes. Tim, a friend of our family, had owned a haberdashery store and lived upstairs. We climbed the steep, narrow stairs to a noisy and confusing scene where we faced Tim, all dressed and apparently asleep in a box bed in the parlor. Mom had explained death and Irish wakes to me on the bus, but I was still uneasy. We knelt beside Tim to say a prayer, and I watched his face to see if he would move. He didn't – he really was dead.

Mom visited, and I wandered around. One room was full of men and two women smoking. When I reached the kitchen, I thought that I, along with Tim, had died and gone to heaven. Every possible dish and treat filled the table and sideboards. I waited for Mom's chocolate cake to reach the kitchen. A woman who smelled like flowers picked me up, placed me in a chair, cut a big piece of Mom's cake, and poured a glass of milk. Savoring the cake and milk, I decided that wakes in general were good ideas after all, especially Irish wakes because of the milk, cake, and other refreshments. But I still had many questions for Mom about death and dying.

"I saw a dead body and ate a big piece of Mom's cake," I bragged to Dave, on our return.

"You lucky guy. All I did was go to school all day," Dave said. "What did Tim look like?"

"He was sleeping in a small box bed, but not breathing, so he was really dead."

"Next time, I want to go and see a dead body and get some cake," Dave whined.

"Jim doesn't go to kindergarten in the afternoon, that's why I took him," Mom said. "Your turn will come." She was careful to practice fairness in parenting. Friends later told Dave and me that we were unusually fair. "People could trust the Cuddy boys to cut a pie evenly," Dave said, reminiscing one day about this trait that we both inherited from Mom.

At about age eight and seven, Dave and I learned a basic religious truth from Mom. We stopped at downtown St. Ambrose Church for a brief prayer. The ancient custodian, Mr. Gunn, was changing the sanctuary candle suspended from the ceiling. He set up a rickety, old stepladder with more arthritis in its wooden joints than in his own, and started up the ladder with the lighted replacement candle in a glass container. The legs of the ladder and the legs of Mr. Gunn began to shake. Dave and I looked at Mom who saw the perilous situation and did a curious thing. She closed her eyes and prayed peacefully.

Dave and I kept watching the drama unfold. Our eyes went back and forth from Mr. Gunn to Mom at prayer. After he had taken out the old candle and put in the new, he started down. When the ladder shook almost uncontrollably, I held my breath until he stepped safely to the floor. Mom opened her eyes and signaled us that it was time to leave. Her immediate prayer had been answered.

"Mom, how old is Mr. Gunn?" Dave asked, on the steps in front of church. Looking back, I guessed that Dave was really asking what just happened with Mr. Gunn and the ladder.

"He must be over eighty," she said and paused. "Boys, somehow at all times, God watches over all of us," she added to interpret the meaning of Mr. Gunn and the rickety ladder.

Throughout the centuries, great minds have spent considerable time on the subject of divine providence. In retrospect, I believe that Mom got it almost right: Somehow God watches over all of us. But I've guessed that if Dad were with us, he would've rushed over and said his prayer while holding the ladder. In my view, God's providence is active in the world, but it requires both prayer and action on our part.

"By the way, your Grandpa Cawley made these sturdy church railings," Mom noted while we were still standing on the church steps. She never missed a chance to pass on family history.

Mom was an excellent listener, and Dad regularly confided in her. Over the years I noticed that relatives and neighbors talked to her by phone or in person about their problems. Mom was non-judgmental and let people find relief by sharing with her their pains and worries. I recalled that she spent a long time on the phone one evening listening to the problems of a friend. After hanging up, Mom muttered a few words, shook her head, and then seemed to put the call entirely out of her mind. Given the education, Mom might've been a counselor or social worker.

The only time I disliked her listening habit was in the winter. I remember a day when Mom, Dave, and I were in Burt's Department Store, and she began visiting with a friend. In our blue snowsuits with the neatly patched knees, we began to heat up, and the feeling of claustrophobia came over me. I looked at Dave, and his face went from pink to red, and he rolled his eyes. After her conversation, she finally led us out into the winter air. I felt like a swimmer saved at the last second by a lifeguard, and Dave looked equally relieved. Even now, decades later that memory makes me gasp.

Mom's role in our family and in life was that of diplomat and peacemaker. I remember her running down our porch steps to break up fights between kids. She generally avoided confrontations and kept the peace in our home. Yet, several times I saw her stand up to Dad. "See here!" she would say strongly. That was the tip-off for Dad, Dave, and me that she meant business.

Our Inherited Traits

"Dave looks like his father, and Jim looks like his mother," observed relatives and neighbors, and even strangers. There was more than physical resemblance. Dave and Dad were confrontational and liked to mix it up with each other and also with others. I followed Mom who was clever at disarming situations and changing the subject.

"Hey, you changed the subject," Dad said to me one day, after I adjusted our talk to a more positive track. "I was just getting warmed up."

"Jim's a diplomat," Mom said often, reinforcing my family script. Dave developed aptitudes for competitive business, and I for the helping professions.

Mom was an excellent cook. She used light seasoning and would be horrified at today's Cajun, Indian, Thai, and other spicy cooking. Some of her specialties were oatmeal square cookies, chocolate cake, apple pie, baked ham, and meat pie with a thick biscuit crust. For some reason she often ordered capon instead of turkey for Thanksgiving.

She had strong ideas about washing dishes and kitchen cleanliness. The three males of her household generally stayed out of her way in the kitchen, her closely guarded turf. We would help her after a big dinner or a late supper, but she was uncomfortable whenever we used cleaning methods different than her own.

Dave and I developed, from parental teaching and example, a love for travel and movies. In 1947, fourteen years after he sold his Model T Ford, Dad bought a forest green Chevrolet sedan. Mom learned to drive right away and was pleased to get her driver's license. No more buses for us. We immediately began a series of trips, short and long. Dad showed Dave and me how to read road maps and route markers. Endicott was the center, and roads ran, like spokes of a wheel, outward in every direction. Our destinations in New York were: Niagara Falls, Thousand Islands, New York City, Cooperstown for the Baseball Hall of Fame, Syracuse for the New York State Fair, and many attractive state parks. We occasionally drove to

Wilkes-Barre to touch Dad's Pennsylvania roots and visit his relatives. We even took longer trips to Atlantic City and Boston and stayed in tourist homes, forerunners of bed and breakfast accommodations, but without the breakfast.

About 1949, we visited Buffalo and then toured Father Baker's Orphanage nearby. Dave and I watched the kids playing in the big yard and didn't notice that Mom and Dad had disappeared for a while. We were oblivious of their true mission. On the way out of Buffalo, they told us that they had applied to adopt an infant girl. Mary Ellen would have been her name.

"'At forty-three, you're too old to be adoptive parents,'" Dad said, quoting the social worker.

"She couldn't make any exceptions," Mom added wistfully, saddened by the outcome.

"Damn bureaucrats!" Dad added, angry at the lack of flexibility.

In the back seat, I looked at Dave and he shrugged – we didn't know what to say. The long ride home seemed like a silent wake for the daughter and sister we almost had. I've sometimes wondered about Mary Ellen, now about fifty-six, and how she would have enriched our family.

Dad shared with us his fondness for movies. He sometimes went to late movies alone on Monday nights. The next day he would report on the plot, and the actors and actresses to Mom, Dave, and me. Sometimes we went to the movies as a family, but more often Dave and I joined the Jackson Avenue gang of boys and rushed to the Saturday matinee. Mom gave each of us two dimes for admission and candy. We tried to buy a child's ticket as long as possible. The ticket seller sometimes grilled us about our ages. In time we were too tall to trick her. Like Dad, we related the details of the movies when we came home.

Dave preferred golfing with his friends and pursued this sport for decades, but I learned from Dad how to fish. Dad, his brothers, and I fished for bass in the nearby Chenango and Tioughnioga Rivers, tributaries of the Susquehanna. Wearing hip boots, we usually waded too far out and had to empty our bulging boots on the shore from time to time. We bought small bullheads or stonies for bait, but sometimes used dobsons or hellgrammites. A dobson with its fat body, tiny legs, and sharp pincers looked to me like an upscale centipede.

Dad usually caught more keepers than his brothers or I did. Like Captain Ahab, he was a relentless fisherman. He casted more times, changed his bait more often, and waded farther into the river than anyone else. I wasn't with Dad on the day he caught the big one, a great smallmouth bass on a dobson. It was a trophy fish by local standards. Dad stopped by *The Binghamton Press*, and the sports editor ran a picture of him with the fish. Dad even had it stuffed and hung it in our attic for decades.

St. Ambrose ~ The Family Anchor

In the immigrant Catholic Church, the local parish was a sturdy anchor, and St. Ambrose Church was central to our parents. They were married there and presented Dave and me for Baptism there. The pastor also asked them to be the communal sponsors for the confirmation class one year. They knew many members of the other families by name.

Mom and Dad followed the tradition of their parents to value the parish church. Mom told of a conversation she had with Grandma Cawley about St. Ambrose parish. "The priests of St. Ambrose, they come and they go, but I remain," Grandma had said to her, in a nostalgic mood. "I recall Father Dwyer coming on horseback from St. James Church in Johnson City to offer Mass for us, the pioneers of Endicott."

"Grandma was a member of St. Ambrose Church for about seventy years," Mom said. Dad and Mom belonged to St. Ambrose Church for over four decades until our family moved to West Endicott in 1951, and we unhappily and reluctantly joined Our Lady of Good Counsel Church.

Joe Cawley, as noted, made and installed the safety railings on the front steps of St. Ambrose Church. He was not an artist skilled in the decorative arts; he was a master plumber, but his railings were functional and sturdy. "I remember when Joe put in those railings. They may have to use dynamite to remove them," Dad said. "Joe Cawley made everything to last."

In my middle years, I experienced a chain reaction of memories. I noticed new railings on the steps of St. Ambrose Church. That reminded me of Mom's family history lesson about Joe's railings. Then I remembered Dad's observations about Joe's handiwork. Then I recalled how Dave and I used to climb and swing on those church railings. As family storyteller, I've found that one memory often leads to other recollections, some connected, some unconnected.

Reflecting on the influence of faith on our family, I recalled a story about premature death. Mom's sister died at forty-four of cancer, and her husband and toddler son survived her death. Aunt Frances Cawley Doyle had been warm and loving toward others. A devout Catholic, she brought a service mentality to her work with families on public assistance. Dave and I enjoyed her company because she was funny and likable; she would mimic a monkey when we entreated her.

Dad and Mom had joined her husband and other family members in keeping watch around her deathbed. Just before she died, her face became radiant. All of those present witnessed her radiant and peaceful death and believed that they saw a divine encounter. This story has been told many times at family gatherings. As storyteller-seanachie, I have no need to try to explain definitively the meaning of every unusual family happening, but I decided to share my tentative opinion. Under God's providence, the radiance of Aunt Frances reinforced for the family the sense that she had been a woman of exceptional character and loving service and that she had journeyed to eternal life. Her premature death marked one of the low points in our family saga, and the radiance phenomenon helped our family to work through grief. But it was not a magical substitution for the lengthy process of grief. Despite the radiance story, Grandma Cawley took a long time to work through the pain of her daughter's premature death, as I related earlier.

A Dream Come True ~ 425 June Street

Dad and Mom's long-deferred dream of owning their own home became a reality in 1951. I recalled that the price for the

71

newly constructed house at 425 June Street was $10,500, and at the last moment, the bank wanted more cash for the down payment. Dad fumed that some bankers, like outlaws in western movies, held up ordinary families, but without even wearing masks. Dave and I came to the rescue with our war/savings bonds from the WWII years.

For Dave and me, the best feature of the new house was the shower. Until then we had only use of a tub. At last, we had a shower and tub. The house was a two-bedroom ranch on a lot near a wild area. Nanticoke Creek split east of our site, rejoined again west of our lot, and left behind a densely wooded island beyond our back property line. We were happy in our own home.

On the day of the official family housewarming party, Joe Cawley and I chatted in front of the only house that my parents ever owned. He was annoyed at the crooked line of trees in the yard.

"Anybody can put two trees in a row," he said. "It takes a craftsman to put three trees in a row. Don't contractors measure anymore?" Dad had claimed that Joe would rip up his work and start again if it didn't meet his personal standards. Joe kept studying those trees that were out of alignment. Anxious that he might rip up the three newly planted trees, the work of another man, I deftly changed the subject.

Whenever I smell cigar smoke, memories flood my mind. Our parents went to an out-of-town wedding with an overnight stay, and Dave staged an unauthorized housewarming party. He invited five of his eleventh grade pals for a poker party with hot pie (pizza to those outside of Endicott) and soda. A box of Dutch Masters cigars was a special feature of the party. I turned in about 11:00 p.m., but when I heard the party ending, I got up to help with the cleaning and cover-up. Two of the guys had arranged to stay over at our house. They gave half-hearted help, and then one fell asleep on my bed, and the other took Dave's bed. Our parents' room was out of bounds. After Dave claimed the couch, I lined the bathtub with several blankets and slept fitfully. The tub wasn't too hard; it was too short.

After a late breakfast, we insisted that the departing guests cart away the hot pie boxes, soda bottles, and a bag of cigar butts and ashes. We then opened all the windows, and the curtains billowed like spinnaker sails. We sprayed air freshener throughout the new house as a final precaution. Our biggest challenge was to overcome Mom's acute sense of smell.

Following a well-rehearsed plan, we lit up cigars in the backyard when we saw Dad and Mom driving toward the garage. After their expected inspection of the new house, they came out to the backyard where Dave and I were puffing away.

"Did you smoke cigars in our new house while we were gone?" Mom questioned.

"Well, we did for a while," Dave responded coolly.

"Then we decided it was better to smoke out here," I quickly added. "How was the wedding?" I said, trying to switch to a more positive subject. Because Mom was an expert at changing the subject, she easily saw through my ploy.

"The wedding was fine, but see here, I'm not finished yet. I'm glad you told the truth, because I smelled cigars inside. And I also smelled room freshener," she added, before turning and going back into the house. From inside the kitchen she called out, "And no more cigars in this new house."

Dad seemed bemused by the scene. He must have had an intuition of the card party from only minimal evidence. "Somebody left these on a row of books in the bookcase," he said to Dave, slipping him a deck of cards and five loose poker chips. Dad walked into the house. I didn't know what Dad was thinking, but maybe he was remembering a time he had pulled a fast one on his mother a generation earlier. Dave and I knew that he would not tell Mom about the card party. Some things mothers don't need to know.

The house on June Street was our delight. Strangers stopped, a few years later, and asked whether our attractive house would be for sale anytime soon. Dad said he would get back to them in a day or two. He discussed the idea with Mom and suggested that we could move to a big apartment near downtown. We could even sell the car and take the bus again. Mom told Dave and me about the proposal.

"Sell the house?" Dave shouted, registering his opposition.

"Sell the car?" I whispered in disbelief.

"I know your father. He couldn't possibly sell this house, our pride and joy, or the car," she said, smiling. After several discussions, Mom and Dad jointly resolved the issue. Mom was right, and their decision was no sale. The house at 425 June St. was their longtime home. Dad lived there for twenty-six years, and Mom for thirty-nine years.

Churchmen thought that the earth was the center of the universe, but Galileo had a wider view. I thought that Dave and I were the center of our parents' world, but I grew to understand that they had a complex web of experiences and memories before we were born. When we left home, they enjoyed their life together and prized several winters in Florida after Dad retired.

"I couldn't stand one more sunny day," Mom said to me, happy to be home after a longer than usual stay in Florida.

They also accompanied me, in their retirement, on one of my trips to Ireland and especially enjoyed scenic drives along the coast. In 1970 we were the first ones in our family's history to return to Ireland since our ancestors fled the Famine. We were probably the first ones able to afford such a distant vacation, and later others eventually went *home* again.

Parents' Passing ~ Eternal Connections

Dad's death was hard. He survived cancer in 1960 and again in 1968, but the disease came back in 1976. He slowly wasted away, and modern medicine kept pain and anxiety at bay. I visited him at Lourdes Hospital one noontime, and Mom was there. Dad was resting with pursed lips and folded hands. I tried to talk with him, but he was in another mental place. I asked Mom to go to the cafeteria.

"What's with the pursed lips and folded hands?" I said over lunch.

"That's something new," she said. I laughed, and that seemed to free her to laugh as well. We kept saying that it wasn't funny, but we kept laughing.

When we returned to the room, Dad was alert, but still had pursed lips and folded hands.

"Here I am in this hospital bed, and I heard from the nurse that you two were gallivanting down in the cafeteria," he said, trying to push our guilt buttons.

Mom winked at me and sprang into action. After forty-four years of marriage she knew just what to say and do. "Well now, we've been asleep at the switch," she said, using an old-time railroad expression to explain our inattention. I watched her fix his pillow, wash his face, and comb his hair. He relaxed his lips and unfolded his hands. Soon they were visiting and holding hands again.

During his long illness Mom went to Lourdes Hospital to visit with him every day. A state trooper stopped her for weaving on the George F. Highway on her way home one winter night; she had started to doze. After he heard her hospital story, he urged her to get some sleep and to take care of her own health. Mom, who never even received a parking ticket, later enjoyed telling about her only brush with the law.

Dad died in 1977, at age seventy. Mom lived another thirteen years with occasional mini-strokes and received much support and help from her sisters, Jule and Loretta, and also from her niece, Joyce. Then Mom suffered a massive stroke at home and never regained consciousness. Dave and I were with her in the hospital when she died quietly, at age eighty-four. Even though we were expecting her death, I felt as if I had taken a fierce blow to my chest.

After the house was sold, I walked through the empty rooms for the last time. It was like an echo chamber, and I heard in my memory the voices of Dave and me playing mini-basketball in the garage, the voice of Dad telling about his trophy fish, and the voice of Mom counseling her many clients on the phone. After forty years, another family with different voices would soon be heard here. I locked the door for the last time, noticed those trees, now tall but still out of perfect alignment, thought of the accurate measurer, Joe Cawley, took one final look, and slowly drove away.

We still miss Dad and Mom. Joyce and I visit their graves at Calvary Cemetery near Endicott from time to time. When there, we also remember Dave and his daughter Carolyn, both buried in the south, and Joyce's deceased parents buried near Troy, New York. One day we found the graves of my grandparents, and after long and patient searching, the large family monument with one bold word, **DEAN**. Mom had indicated to me that both Great-grandfather James Dean, Civil War veteran, and Margaret Dean, benign matriarch, were buried there.

Joyce and I don't find cemeteries morbid or sad. I've lingered lately at family graves because I heard or thought I heard the family spirits making music with uilleann pipes and bodhran drums. Were these faint reprises of my enchanted-religious-literary experience on top of the Kerry Reeks? Perhaps. And why shouldn't joyful music be heard at cemeteries? I believe that our deceased family members shared in the Easter victory of Jesus and I believe that one day Joyce and I shall be with them and Joyce's ancestors as part of the complex mystery of eternal life.

It's common today to blame personal problems on one's parents, especially in regard to their style of parenting. Dad and Mom did well in guiding Dave and me through the Depression, schooling, and the tempests of teen years. When I've noticed niece Becky of the sixth generation and other modern soccer moms in designer slacks juggling schedules of life and work, I admire them. I also admired Mom and her generation of mothers, parenting in print dresses, in slower ways, and in simpler times.

Mom sometimes parented indirectly, and Dave and I had to read between her lines. Dad parented more directly. He allowed us more freedom and taught us that the world was positive, not threatening. My summary was that Mom and Dad did their best in imperfectly raising and freeing us. How else do parents practice the art of parenting, except imperfectly? Mom and Dad lived responsibly, died with dignity, and modeled for us how we might do the same.

In the next chapter, the impact of family and education on the growth and development of Dave and me is fleshed out in a series of mostly lighthearted stories blended with some harsh realism. World War II played a significant role in our formation because it was a comprehensive experience. Despite our young ages, we became veterans of the home front.

"We have many photos of Veronica growing up and wearing attractive outfits. Dave saw her as a princess in her family." 1912.

"They had wanted to marry sooner,
but the Depression delayed them for four years."
John and Veronica, on Model T Ford, 1932.

"Mom was an excellent listener…. Given the education,
Mom might've been a counselor or social worker." 1931.

"At one point, John became 'AAAGM-IBM-E,' Administrative
Associate to the Assistant General Manager of IBM-Endicott."
Here Dad worked at the outdoor IBM 100% Club Convention,
1949.

Chapter Five

Fifth Generation:
World War II Home Front Generation, 1935

"It appears that the disremembrance of World War Two is as disturbingly profound as the forgettery of the Great Depression: World War Two, an event that changed the psyche as well as the face of the United States and of the world."

Studs Terkel, The Good War, An Oral History of World War II

Fifth Generation: Two Brothers

David M. Cuddy	James J. Cuddy
Veteran of Home Front	Veteran of Home Front
Favored Navy	Favored Marines

Our Younger Days ~ Huck Finn and Tom Sawyer

This longest chapter could be called "Memory and Memories" and was easiest to write because it dealt with stories from my generation. Dave Cuddy was born on September 5, 1935, near Endicott. He had an unusual memory and told of pre-kindergarten events. He recalled that at about age four he climbed out a small window onto the roof of the front porch. When Mom saw him from the yard, she ran into the house and up the stairs to the front bedroom.

"Dave, come in," she whispered, "Dave, come in." His action and her soft-spoken plea were illustrative: Dave sometimes tested limits, and Mom was a gentle parent. She confirmed his memories of that event.

On November 14, 1936, I was born in Endicott. My memory goes back to kindergarten, but I've had to work at recalling childhood stories. When I gently and patiently squeezed the sponge of my memory, recollections gradually dripped, dripped, dripped from head, to typing fingers, to computer screen. Because Dave and I were only fourteen months apart, I remembered that I spent much of my early life trying to keep up with him. After morning kindergarten, I would spy with envy through the window on Dave's higher education in the first grade. I noticed that he and his classmates were orderly.

In kindergarten, we were far less civilized. The boys pushed and shoved at opening bell to get to the first chair to the left of Mrs. Brundage, and the girls tried to get to the first chair to her right. We sat in a semicircle. I vaguely recalled that the winners were alpha male and alpha female for the day, no more struggling until the next morning. The scrambling for chairs puzzled me because there was no fighting for chairs in our small family.

Dave listened to my complaint and coached me in the offensive and defensive tactics of pushing and shoving. After his training, I was sometimes able to fight my way to the first chair. Looking back, I concluded that I naively went to kindergarten to learn to read. I never expected such Darwinian challenges, but I survived with the fittest of our class. However, first grade was more civilized.

Mom saved a newspaper picture of Dave and his classmates in their first grade stage program. It was a spring show, and the children were dressed as flowers with Dave in the first row. This picture prompted me to recall a stage program from when I was in second grade. Classmate Rose Marie and I joined others in a children's version of the minuet. Butterflies filled my stomach before the curtain opened, but they flew away at the first notes of the music. With no sisters and mostly boys in our neighborhood, I had limited interaction with girls, but I remembered that dancing with her was fun. Rose Marie and I reminisced about our minuet, fifty-eight years later, at a millennium reunion.

Henry B. Endicott Public School was only eight houses from our home, and I recalled feeling morning exhilaration on the short walk to school. Mom saved our report cards, and my second grade card from 1943 showed the basics of reading, writing, and arithmetic, plus add-ons of spelling, art, and English. The conduct side of the card had no marks for me about cooperation, courtesy, effort, promptness, dependability, neatness, or posture; no news was good news.

My review of the ancient report card evoked more memories. Around third or fourth grade, I began, in the unformed and naïve ways of a child, to develop the instincts of a writer. On occasion I thought of the sun as a basketball or beach ball or dodge ball, forming my first similes. I would later learn about literary devices and other implements in the toolbox of a writer. When I wrote a child's report about World War II, the teacher read it to the class. I was pleased, but soon learned the importance of an elephantine skin for a writer. A surly classmate sought me out and said, "That stunk." It was my first experience of a blunt critic.

By fourth grade, we became rambunctious, and our teacher warned us that the punishment for serious misbehavior was hard time in the custodian's dark storeroom. This black hole became the subject of many rumors.

"I've heard many spooky things about the dark punishment room," I said to Dave.

"Don't believe everything you hear," he said, always one step ahead of me.

Two of our classmates did hard time in the black hole, but they wouldn't give us any of the details about the allegedly black-as-midnight room. They probably grew into tough marines who would have no trouble in giving only name, rank, and serial number if captured in war. I always stared at the windowless door of that room as we passed it on the way to the gym. One day, I noticed that the door was ajar and light was streaming out. I knew then that the black hole was a hoax. I didn't tell Dave of my discovery because I didn't want to give him the satisfaction of being right. I lost innocence not by one event, but gradually.

It was not all school and no play. Before computer games, play was simpler. A photo showed Dave and me in almost matching cowboy suits in 1940 – we looked like tiny versions of Roy Rogers and Gene Autry. I recalled that Dave later was The Lone Ranger and I was Tonto, again with costumes. I didn't always know the details of my roles and tried to match Dave's more refined play skills. We also played with boys from Jackson Avenue. Gus was an American with Mexican background, the England brothers were English and Irish, Carlo's heritage was Italian, and Dave and I carried Irish genes. The melting pot boiled with even richer diversity in school.

A few years ago I walked around our old neighborhood. I wandered through the streets east of the old school and noted the development. In our day, there were overgrown meadows and thickets that we called "the swamp." That stroll triggered memories of blackberry picking in one area more open to the sun. One hot August afternoon, Dave and I, perhaps nine and eight, were gradually filling kitchen pots with plump wild blackberries and drifted toward some backyard fences.

"Boys, you can't pick berries there," a homeowner yelled from his chair in the shade of his porch.

"We're way beyond your fence line," Dave shouted back, true to form by testing the man's authority and escalating the situation.

"Wait right there," he said, moving toward the gate in his wooden fence. "I'm coming over to take those berries."

"What'll we do?" I asked anxiously, looking longingly into my pail. The blackberries came to within six inches of the brim.

"Let's run to the swamp," Dave whispered. "Follow me."

"Stop, boys, stop!" the man hollered, running after us.

I was afraid he would catch us, but we quickly disappeared into our swamp where we knew every path. Even the National Guard couldn't find us there. We caught our breath, checked the berries, and figured our losses. While running, we both lost a few berries from our pots, but not enough to leave a telltale trail. Like Huck Finn and Tom Sawyer, we reveled in the adventure. Mom was glad to receive our ripe berries and made two pies. During dessert Dave and I giggled a few times, and Dad and Mom knew that something had happened, but they didn't ask any questions. Their wise parenting included the ability to overlook as well as to oversee.

About this time, Dave was the main character in a story of parental oversight. He went on a partial hunger strike and wouldn't eat his lima beans. Dad, overplaying his hand, gave him an ultimatum, "You can't leave the table till you eat those lima beans."

"After all, children are starving in China," Mom chimed in, adding a layer of guilt.

Going out to the yard, I noticed that Dave was still at the table, Dad was listening to the radio, and Mom was reading the newspaper. I played catch with Norm from next-door until Dave finally came out.

"What happened, Dave? Did you eat the beans?"

"Everything is okay." Those three words were the only thing he said. I suspected there might be more to the story.

Three months later, workmen came to install a replacement refrigerator. Dave didn't seem interested and hurried toward Gus's house. I watched as they carried the old fridge down the porch stairs and hoisted the new one onto the porch. Mom was in the kitchen with broom and pan and swept out the accumulated dust and cobwebs. She discovered the dried lima beans and called me to see the shriveled remains. When Mom laughed, I felt it was okay for me to laugh. Our parents may have decided that Dave already did his time. Whatever the reason, he escaped further punishment. This story we told again and again.

World War II ~ A Two Front War

World War II was the central event of the twentieth century in my judgment. Tom Brokaw wrote about the importance of the front line and also the home front in his popular book *The Greatest Generation*: "Any war has at least two fronts: the front line, where the fighting is done, and the home front, which provides the weapons, the supplies, the transportation, the intelligence, the political and moral support. The home front rarely gets equal credit, but World War II required such a massive buildup in such a short time, the home front effort was as impressive as the fighting in Europe or the Pacific." WWII was an all-encompassing experience even for those who lived through the war at home.

"Boys, we are at war with Germany and Japan," Dad told Dave and me when we were six and five. He explained for us the attack on Pearl Harbor in terms we could understand. I didn't recall this specific conversation from my kindergarten year of 1941, but Dave talked about it many times.

Often in the course of writing this book, I noticed how events in my youth are mirrored in the present. For example, in 2001, parents all over America, like Dad after Pearl Harbor, were trying to explain to their children the terrorist attacks in New York and Washington, and the plane crash in Pennsylvania. Teachers and psychologists were on television suggesting ways for parents to deal with the horrifying images of airplanes crashing into tall buildings that were seared on the minds of their children. Parents wanted to know how best to give children the assurance of safety.

Dad was patriotically concerned about the war, and turned down by the local draft board for being too old at thirty-seven, he made a special train trip to New York City with a friend to try to enlist in the Navy there. "Go back and work on the home front," the recruiter said. "You're too old for active duty." Dad came home frustrated and told us the details. When he was at work, Mom, Dave, and I admitted that we were glad about the age limit.

Random recollections of WWII and the home front came back to me. Dave had his booklets to fill with war bond stamps on sale at school, and I had mine. We received war/savings bonds for completed booklets. As I already mentioned, these bonds helped Dad and Mom buy our first house, six years after the war. Food rationing also involved special stamps. As soon as Mom heard a wildfire rumor of scarce items on the shelves of the A&P Market, she sent Dave or me racing there with appropriate stamps. During the war, we developed a taste for margarine because butter was scarce. For years after the war, I felt vaguely unpatriotic for eating butter. Even though we still didn't have a car, I recalled gas rationing. Those with jobs essential to the war effort and public safety had priority stamps on their windshields for more gas per month, and ordinary drivers had regular classification for limited gas.

We saved kitchen grease in cans for the war, and I never understood why. Customers could get in free at The Lyric Movie Theater, one Saturday, with a certain weight of scrap metal.

"Joe, we need some scrap metal for the war and to get in free at the movies," Dave said.

"Follow me." We watched him root around in his storage area for loose metal ends. Grandpa Joe found some pipe ends for Dave and me. His plumbing pipes, in reversal of the Bible saying about beating swords into plowshares, were beaten into guns.

I also recalled "victory gardens" that home front patriots were urged to plant in yards to increase food production. Dad grew a flourishing vegetable garden during the war. Some gardens around town looked like Dust Bowl plots with short rows of parched and spindly plants. It was obvious that some citizens didn't have green thumbs, but they tried. Dad and Mom pointed out to us the signs of Gold Star Parents hanging in some home windows to indicate the death of a son or daughter in the war. At an early age, Dave and I learned that real people on both sides died in WWII.

Dad volunteered to be an air raid warden and received a white pith helmet and a long flashlight. He checked to make sure the lights were out in our neighborhood during air raid drills. Workers had painted the windows black at IBM and Endicott-Johnson, lest the factories be easily seen from the air at night. IBM had three shifts and made many technical war machines. E-J manufactured Army boots, vital for the foot soldiers, so both factories were probable targets for enemy bombs. Dave and I were excited about occasional air raid drills.

"Where are the enemy planes?" I kept asking Dave in our darkened house during a raid.

"It's just a test, and there aren't any planes," he said, giving me the look reserved for those ignorant of serious war issues. Luckily for us, enemy planes never came to bomb IBM, E-J, and our house only six blocks from the factories.

War on Film ~ Impact on Children

In retrospect, I judged that the severest impact of WWII on Dave and me came from film. In vicarious ways, we witnessed violent scenes of war at the movie theaters in weekly newsreels, feature war movies, and occasional documentaries such *as The March of Time.* Of course, British, Polish, Russian, Italian, German, Dutch, French, Chinese, Japanese, and other children of our age experienced WWII directly with real planes and real bombs.

Newsreels of the liberation of concentration camps were especially horrifying. Our generation will never doubt the facts and scope of the Jewish Holocaust, the knowledge of which completed our loss of innocence. Jews of all ages endured the torments of imprisonment, and six million Jews were exterminated in the camps. I learned later that Elie Wiesel survived the camps and Anne Frank died there. Who can fully understand the different life spans of these two against the background of absolute Nazi evil? As an adult, they symbolized for me the unfathomable mystery of the living and the dead, and the survivors and those who perished.

Margaret Bourke-White, famous photographer for *Life* magazine, captured WWII on film. Vicki Goldberg wrote about the life of Bourke-White and the impact of her photography during the war: "Pictures like Margaret's made Americans believe in the Nazi atrocities for the first time; they could not be denied. Newsreels showed the camps to hushed audiences. Buchenwald, Belsen, Dachau – their images were etched in memory forever." Those etchings remained vivid in my memory, and I easily recalled the naked bodies of hundreds of dead Jews stacked like cords of wood. The fleeing Nazi soldiers had been unable to burn these bodies in the ovens. And I could see in memory the pictures of survivors with their ribs visible. Some violence children should not see, but Dave and I, in fourth and third grades at the end of the war, witnessed so many graphic atrocities in newsreels that we aged before our time.

When in Amsterdam, a few years ago, Joyce and I made sure we visited the Anne Frank Home and Museum. Every day a line of people wound its way around the block to see this vivid microcosm of WWII. Moving slowly we climbed to the hideout behind the bookcase. A hush came upon us as we pondered the meaning of the Holocaust through the eyes of one engaging Jewish teenager and her family and neighbors.

In 1945, on Victory in Europe Day (V-E Day) and Victory over Japan Day (V-J Day), we were jubilant and exhilarated. On each occasion, our family stopped by St. Ambrose Church for thanksgiving and then surged up and down Washington Avenue in the crowd hysterical with joy and relief. Later there was a final victory parade with workers from E-J, IBM, and other smaller companies marching in step and bursting with pride. Dave and I, along with other kids from Jackson Avenue, watched the parade from the roof of the furniture store. I don't remember how we merited rooftop seating; maybe we shimmied up the back drainpipe.

Veterans of the shooting war were returning home, and homecomings were emotional events. Norman Rockwell crafted a famous magazine cover of a soldier returning home and the whole neighborhood spontaneously welcoming him. One of my Mother's cousins survived a German prisoner-of-war camp. Dad's brother came home from the Navy and brought us a small piece of a Japanese kamikaze plane. It crashed just short of his aircraft carrier, The Bennington, and its wing flipped up to the flight deck. Dave had hoped to be a sailor, and I a marine, but the war ended in 1945. We were seasoned veterans of the home front, but we received no special celebration. Relieved that WWII was finally over, we turned to the normal phases of growing up.

Parochial School ~ Forced Enrollment

A popular priest gave a strong sell in his Sunday sermon about taking advantage of St. Ambrose School for grades one through nine. Dad and Mom decided to enroll Dave and me. We had no warning and were shocked, yes, shocked. We tried every strategy and ploy to stay in public school, but Dad and Mom wouldn't rescind their order.

"You poor guys," Gus said, leading the neighborhood boys who resembled the friends of Job.

"Why do you have to go downtown when there's a public school right here?" Norm asked.

"Those Sisters wear funny hats," Ed noted, prompting laughter.

"You poor guys," repeated Gus.

"We've tried everything, but our parents won't budge," Dave said.

"You better think of something soon," Ken advised.

"Yeah, Labor Day and the opening of school are next week," I said.

"You poor guys," Gus said, summing up the looming disaster for Dave and me.

Dave had enough from Gus and wrestled him to the ground. "This is for being such a 'Gloomy Gus,'" Dave said, punching his arm. Gus reacted with his infectious laugh.

Dave and I adjusted to parochial school, our new classmates, and the Daughters of Charity. With their dramatic French peasant hats of a different era, they glided like swans into school and church. It's now fashionable to take cheap shots at parochial schools and to depict Sisters as strict, grim, and merciless teachers, but we were able to appreciate their human side.

Dave and I especially liked Sister Pierre who was warm and friendly. Decades later I was able to contact her by mail; I had learned that she reverted to her family name of Sister Mary Frances Cumberland after the reforms of the Second Vatican Council. She sent supportive letters to us. I later sent a Christmas card and note to Sister Mary Frances, but another sister responded with news of her death. Dave and I were glad we had contacted her before it was too late.

We soon made new friends and became happy students at St. Ambrose, but we wouldn't admit it to Dad and Mom during the first year. We made them pay for their lightning strike decision. I can't say whether Mom and Dad saw through our first year's false front.

Going home from fifth grade, two classmates – I remember vaguely Dusty and Carlo – and I passed The First Methodist Church. In a spirit of mischief, we rapped on the back of the outside sign, which caused the letters to fall to the bottom of the frame, and ran away. A week later, emboldened by the success of our first prank, we snuck into the vestibule and looked around.

"That must ring the church bell," I observed, pointing to a rope dangling from a hole in the ceiling.

"No, not a good idea to ring it," Dusty said, providing conventional wisdom.

"Too dangerous," Carlo added, by way of a quick risk assessment.

"We'll get caught," I said, in a spirit of realism. "It's broad daylight."

After a long pause, we suddenly pushed and shoved and jumped for the rope, but couldn't reach it. While two knelt on all fours, the third stood on their backs and tolled the bell a few times. First Dusty, then Carlo, then I took a turn. We ran four blocks before we stopped to laugh, but we should've known for whom the bell tolled. It tolled for us.

A busybody saw us flee the church and called the minister who then phoned our pastor, Father Hopkins. "You must apologize for rapping the sign and ringing the church bell. And don't forget that you represent St. Ambrose School in Endicott," he said. We didn't think of ourselves as Catholic commandos on a raid against religious rivals. We were just mischievous.

A year later, Halloween gave us license for more mischief. "We're going to tie some costumed kid to a tree," Dave said, "and other spooky stuff."

I told my friends what Dave and his seventh grade pals were planning to do with their rope, and we decided it was a good plan to imitate. By then we had outgrown the wearing of costumes and were more concerned with tricks than treats. My friends and I loosely tied a boy, known to us (a big mistake) and dressed as Superman, to a telephone pole.

"Listen Superman, there are many trick-or-treaters so you'll be set free in minutes," I whispered, feeling a pang of guilt. We left him at the stake and ran down the street.

"Superman will be avenged," he called after us, really into his role. "You'll see."

Superman's father took our trick seriously and went to the police. The next day, detectives came to our house with a list of all the suspects. Again we had to apologize, this time to the boy and his father. "See here, Jim, the excuse of boys being boys is wearing thin," Mom scolded.

"It's hilarious that our tied-up cowboy didn't tell and your Superman did," Dave said later. "So much for 'The Man of Steel.'"

Two years later, Dad received a summons to bring Dave to a hearing; Sister Matilde of the ninth grade had sent the note home. She was a firm teacher. Mom and I waited at home for the verdict. "Justice was swift," Dad reported. "She claimed Dave was a ringleader of hooligans."

"What else?" Mom asked.

"That's what's puzzling. The trial was brief, and the sentence was handed down quickly: 'No more cops and robbers.'"

Dave decided to cut short the story and said, "Okay, no more cops and robbers." When Dad laughed, Mom and I laughed. Dave took that as a sign that the case was closed. He jumped on his bike and rode away.

Basketball ~ Obsession

Basketball, basketball, basketball. We played informally, in every season, in a small area next-door where Mr. England had put up a backboard, hoop, and even a net. His four sons included Dave and me and other neighborhood boys in games played with their old, mud-stained frayed ball. On Christmas, Dave and I received a joint gift of a bright orange basketball. We decided to limit its use to pickup games at the school gym on off-hours; our new ball was too special to use on the frozen or muddy next-door court. Because the neighborhood guys knew we were holding back the new ball, we weren't picked for any games for two days. Our pantry window suddenly opened, on the third day, and the new ball flew out. I don't recall whether Dad or Mom sized up the situation and acted, but Dave and I were back in the game. Within a year our ball was worn like car tires driven thousands of miles on dirt roads.

Father Moriarity coached us well in the fundamentals of basketball. All boys from grades six to nine could play on intramural teams named for Catholic colleges. Dave and I went on to play for the St. Ambrose team against other parochial schools in the county. Before the games, Father Coach gave a pep talk and reminded us to chatter to distract an opposing foul shooter and also to fall backwards in an exaggerated reaction when an opponent charged or bumped us. A referee once whispered to me, "You can skip the dramatics." While these tactics weren't against the rules, I've wondered whether they fostered sportsmanship. We also went on trips to play at Waverly in New York and Susquehanna in Pennsylvania.

Dave and I were also altar boys who fractured the Latin prayers. This role prompted others and me to consider pursuing a priestly vocation. I asked a parish priest twice during school about the seminary, but I was too distracted by school, basketball, and teen life to focus clearly on plans for the future.

Healthy Sexuality ~ Discovering Girls, Sex Ed 101

As we entered the boy-girl attraction years, we attended school dances. All of the boys stuck together, like football players in a huddle at one end of the gym, and the girls clung together at the other end. At last, drawn by nature's hormones, we danced tentatively and clumsily and were sometimes sweaty-palmed and tongue-tied in the dancing embrace. With a priest or sister as chaperone, we were in little danger of taking liberties and were vague about what liberties were anyway. Through dancing I came to appreciate that girls were soft, fragrant, attractive, and interesting conversationalists. From school dances onward, strictly male bonding lost its luster for Dave and me. We both had a few girlfriends in junior and senior high school, but I'll leave it at that.

About the time of seventh grade for me, two boys in a fight in the backyard next-door shouted the F-word six times, if memory served me well, once as a noun, twice as an adjective, and three times as a verb. Their words were so loud and shrill that they traveled south to the back wall of the A&P market, bounded north to the public school, and then took short bounces to every house in between. Dad ran out the porch to hear, and Mom put down her paper to listen. Dave and I heard the obscene word in different grammatical forms echoing throughout the neighborhood, but these words were part of street life, and we weren't surprised. We feigned deafness in front of Mom and thought our ruse worked.

"See here, obscene words are not allowed in our neighborhood," Mom said later.

"The parents on Jackson Avenue are on a mission," Dave predicted. "You'll see."

We knew that earlier in the year the Sisters had held a meeting of parents of the upper grade students and gave them literature on sex education so we had been expecting something. The echoing F-word triggered Dad to give the Sex Ed. 101 talk a few days later, and maybe other parents gave similar talks. Looking back, I felt he did a positive job by covering the basics. I've since wondered why Dad, with a father-in-law plumber, didn't use examples from Joe's cellar, such as pipes and couplings, for the physical facts of life. He ended on high notes about healthy and normal sexuality and positive values, which probably came from the literature of the Sisters and was avant-garde for those days.

"Well, boys, any questions?" he asked, with a fine sweat on his forehead.

"No, Dad, no questions," we said in unison. Dad was relieved, Dave was relieved, and I was relieved, as I rode Dave's coattails into another stage of development.

One lasting memory of parochial school days was when the school gym served as a theater. Many of the Sisters came from Irish-American backgrounds and staged an Irish minstrel show with Dave's ninth grade and my eighth grade participating. Dave was Mr. Interlocutor. He wore a green long-tailed suit and bantered with Gaelic end men who didn't wear traditional black face, because it would have been offensive. The Sisters wrote the script; some of the jokes were old chestnuts while others were clever. The choral songs – most of us were wearing green in the chorus and seated in a semicircle – ranged from Irish favorites to catchy new ones. Dad, Mom, and I thought that Dave stole the show and enjoyed watching him in multiple performances.

Glued to the Screens ~ Movies and TV

During our school days, movies were a large part of growing up. I estimated that Dave and I saw about 700 films from kindergarten to the end of high school. Like our coal miner ancestors at the end of a shift, we blinked our way into the sunshine of the real world at the end of the movies. The impact was immediate; as youngsters, we rode horses home after westerns and shot our way home after WWII movies. We also ate great quantities of candy and popcorn during those hours in the dark, and some guys risked throwing the empty boxes from the balcony in the Lyric Theater onto those below. Mr. Dietrich, the manager, was so watchful that he usually spotted the culprits and sent them home. The safer Strand Theater had no balcony.

Our love for movies carried over to our adult years. Dave and I enjoyed discussing and recommending movies. A decade ago, we, along with others, made lists of our top ten movies. If Dad were alive, he would have enjoyed participating in this informal survey. Dave ranked the best of his favorites: *The Treasure of the Sierra Madre* (1948), *The Defiant Ones* (1958), and *The Deer Hunter* (1978). The best of the best for me: *Casablanca* (1942), *The Quiet Man* (1952), and *Radio Days* (1987). My pick of *The Quiet Man* now seems uncritical, because some scenes were unfair to women, but overall I enjoyed the broad humor. Just as John Wayne went back to his family origins in Ireland, I returned to my roots at the top of MacGillycuddy's Reeks. Maureen O'Hara was also wonderful in her role.

Just before high school, television arrived to compound the impact of images on our formative minds; movies and television competed for our attention. The Airport Inn on a high hill north of Endicott brought in a snowy TV picture from some distant transmitter, and Dad took us there a few times to watch TV through the electronic blizzard on the screen and to munch on fried chicken. We later watched TV programs on a set in the window of the appliance store on Washington Ave. We even watched with umbrellas in the rain. The sound was piped outside to the crowd. The owner was toying with us because he knew that all the residents of Endicott would buy a 3-channel TV set sooner or later. Dad bought one about 1950 for us to enjoy exciting new entertainment and educational possibilities, and I sensed in retrospect to get out of the rain.

"I remember early TV programs: *Kukla, Fran and Ollie*, *What's My Line?*, *Texaco Star Theater*, and pro-football games. We watched hours, weeks, months, and eventually years of television," I said to Joyce when we discussed the impact of TV.

She shared pleasant memories of early TV days and recalled appearing on the local *Freddy Freihoffer Show* near her home.

Around 1990, Joyce and I attended a St. Ambrose School reunion. It was a Fortieth Gala, but included several classes. I sent some memorabilia ahead, and others did the same. Sister Helen Kelly, a favorite schoolteacher, attended, and each class tried to coax her to sit at its table. However, she diplomatically split her time and sat at each table. School reunions stimulated my retrieval of old memories.

Union-Endicott High School ~ The Melting Pot

When we entered high school and left behind our parochial school days, Dave and I had to readjust to public education where more freedom was allowed. Mrs. Ryan, a teacher at the school and friend of my mother, warned me that incoming students from St. Ambrose School sometimes got into trouble by acting up in the freer atmosphere. She was right. Like Dave before me, I received a few detention slips in my first year. I remember many opportunities in high school for learning, sports, and experiencing the positive dynamics of the melting pot. UEHS was a wonderful place for me.

The Sisters had coached us to request Mrs. Fredricks for Geometry and Miss Hollister for Latin because they were master teachers. Both of my requests were honored, and I was not disappointed.

"Every year several of my students get 100% on the final Geometry test, or else," Mrs. Fredricks told us. Like a drill sergeant, she whipped us into mathematical shape. Carlo Evangelisti and others fulfilled her prophecy by scoring 100% on the state final exam in June.

Miss Hollister, with her degree from nearby Cornell University, perfectly reflected the value of a liberal arts education, and I enjoyed her teaching style and Latin courses. I took four years of Latin in case I ever tried the seminary. One of the toughest football players in the history of UEHS, Fran Angeline, was also a dedicated Latin scholar with her guidance. After Colgate University, he returned to UE, coached football, and taught Latin for decades. A few years ago, Fran wrote a book, *This Tiger's Tale*, about his successful career in coaching (Brundage Publishing, Binghamton, New York).

Union-Endicott High School had over 1,200 students. Dave had already developed his own circle of high school friends, and I enlarged my circle upon entering UEHS. We both had ethnic Catholic friends, Jewish friends, and also white Anglo-Saxon Protestant friends. I never liked the term WASP. There were no African-Americans in Endicott then, to our loss. We studied together, played sports together, went to proms together, and worked out the kinks of adolescence together. Our different ethnic and religious backgrounds blended with one another, and we grew from these valuable interactions.

Dave and I, from this time on, increasingly went our separate ways. The Huck Finn and Tom Sawyer days were over. He put some of his energy into running the quarter mile race for the high school team, and I continued CYO basketball. Even though St. Ambrose School ended with the ninth grade, the parish had a team in the CYO league for high school players. After fifteen years as my tutor, mentor, and adviser, Dave was relieved to give up these roles, and I was happy to be on my own. I owed him for help with the pushing and shoving in kindergarten and other boyhood lessons. I never discovered how Dave, only fourteen months older, knew so much about growing up. Perhaps the burden of the firstborn child is to be savvy and to advise siblings.

During high school, several of us, all males, discovered a secluded spot along Nanticoke Creek for bare ass swimming; our term has been euphemized to B.A. swimming or skinny dipping. We didn't bother with towels, but dried in the sun.

"Boys, cover up. I'm coming along the path," a matronly voice called out one day. Laughing and hooting, we dove into the water and floated like escaping apples in a Halloween tub. In flowing dress and sun hat, she resembled Katherine Hepburn in the film *The African Queen*. As she walked by with averted eyes, we could see her red face. One witty friend later said, "Her blush was redder than a whippoorwill's beak in plum picking time." He must've been saving that quip for months. We sometimes chose to skinny dip in addition to using several public swimming pools in the Triple Cities. Looking back, I decided that it was a healthy rite of male passage and wonderfully cool to the nether regions.

Because few students had cars in our day, we depended on hitchhiking around the Triple Cities, and drivers were generous in picking us up. Dave and his friends, shod in white buck shoes, hitched to Scranton, seventy miles distant, for a lark. They ended up in an industrial section where the local toughs taunted them with special ridicule for their white bucks. My guess was they considered white shoes to be impractical, or elitist, or effete, or all three. The Endicotters jogged to safer ground and thumbed home early. Dave was annoyed at the inhospitable treatment.

As seniors, classmate Bill Hartquist and I hitched 200 miles to New York City and toured there for a few days. On another occasion, friend Fran Fetsko and I hitched to Albany and then on to Boston. On our return, we were at a crossroads with the early April sun falling. We had to decide whether to risk thumbing straight through the Catskill Mountains or to go the longer way via Albany. We chose the safer and longer route, because we didn't want to risk standing throughout a cold night in the remote mountains. We stayed in an old motel beyond Albany and discovered a few insects in the beds in the morning, which was funny to us at the time. However, hitchhiking today is dangerous and not recommended. We grew up in simpler days.

Our St. Ambrose parish basketball team played very well during our high school years. After a senior season of seventeen wins and four losses, we faced arch rival St. Patrick's team in a three-game playoff. We had been playing against the same guys since seventh grade and knew them well. Sometimes we hitchhiked to Binghamton to hang around, smoke cigars, and shoot pool with our foes, but I remember that they never thumbed a ride to Endicott to hang around with us. Because they lived in the city of Binghamton, they seemed to me to project cosmopolitan and urbane airs, and to look down on us as unsophisticates from the village of Endicott with its many factories and malodorous tanneries. It was always doubly sweet to me when we beat them.

In 1990, I discovered a scrapbook in the family attic about our senior basketball season and guessed that Dad had made it. The newspaper clippings were like dried autumn leaves and had to be handled gingerly. There was also a two-generation photo from the paper; I was shooting and Dad was in the bleachers behind me. This picture and the clippings evoked many positive memories of CYO basketball. In the playoff series, St. Pat's won the first game forty-seven to forty-one. We won the second game in overtime sixty-five to sixty-four, and their tall man, John Clark, scored twenty-six points. I presume that we must have focused on containing Clark for the final game.

Before I turned the page, I tried to recall who won that championship game thirty-six years earlier. I soon remembered sharing in a scene of great jubilation. Turning the page, I found that we led nineteen to eighteen at half time and indeed won the final game, beating our cosmopolitan and urbane foes forty-two to thirty. Even the most fragile of records are godsends for a family storyteller.

Our class of 1954 had over 350 students. In our senior year, we strode like dukes and duchesses through the halls of UEHS. We believed our unique class of '54 was like a vintage year in the nearby Finger Lakes wineries. We were sure that our class was filled to the brim with unforgettable characters, and we mythologized one another into heroes and heroines. We gave new meaning to the term *hubris*.

Local class leaders, such as Joe Brill, have tracked down and invited almost all classmates to positive reunions at least five times in the last fifty years. Joe has used his computer to find the missing. Many had moved to distant IBM locations and elsewhere. Nothing has been as effective as recent reunions to demythologize our class. By the millennium reunion, gray hair was the norm for both women and men, and some males, myself included, couldn't conceal bulging midriffs. We may still dream of ourselves as strutting dukes and duchesses, but the reunion pictures and our own hard-earned wisdom gave more accurate readings. I've always been saddened by the updated list of deceased classmates – Greg Fusco died in a nuclear submarine. Ray Tiberi supported a favorite charity, and after his death, Fran

Fetsko and others hold a yearly golf tournament to remember him and further his charity.

Memory Switch ~ Sometimes On, Sometimes Off

Memory has been a fascinating subject for me as storyteller. I concluded that the organic human memory with its emotional component is more subtle, mysterious, and powerful than the cold and unfeeling memory in the metallic, electronic IBM computer. Why did I, decades after high school, remember some classmates and events and not others? At the millennium reunion, Joyce and I chatted with Rose Marie Hospodor. I had scanned my yearbook before the dinner dance and noticed a handwritten note from her in my book indicating that she recalled dancing the minuet with me and others in early grade school.

"Do you remember the minuet in second grade?" I asked, testing her memory, forty-six years after the yearbook and fifty-eight years after second grade.

"Minuet? What minuet?" she asked, drawing a blank. I told her about scanning my yearbook and finding her note about our dance on stage in early grammar school.

"Oh, now I remember the minuet, but a turnabout is fair play. In preparation for tonight I also scanned my yearbook. You wrote, 'The horn blows at midnight' in my book. Do you recall that episode?"

"No memory of that," I admitted, feeling sheepish.

"We went on a date, and after you drove back to my house around midnight, the horn on your Dad's car started beeping intermittently, and you couldn't stop it. One by one the lights in my neighborhood came on, and then the lights in my house went on."

"Yes, now I remember." The day after the reunion, I further recalled that I drove home with on and off beeping down Main Street, Page Avenue, and June Street. But I couldn't remember whether the horn precluded any romantic exchanges.

Memory was always a complex puzzle to me, and I'm comfortable with not completely solving the mysteries of recollection in this book. My memory has served up so many joys in my lifetime that I've easily forgiven it for any lapses or blanks, especially as I've grown older. We call memory difficulties "senior moments" today.

After reviewing my first eighteen years, for this book I wanted to rank ten formative influences on my growing up, and I wish Dave were still alive so I could've polled him. I found the challenge a mixed bag of apples, oranges, and the whole fruit salad. Even so, I pushed myself to rank them because I felt it strengthened my storytelling. My unscientific and subjective ranking of forces, in descending order: family life including Dave's tutorials, public and parochial schools, parish church, movies, WWII home front, early TV, the family car since 1947, basketball, a bemused sense of the universe, and in last place my mythologizing of Endicott into a magical place.

The last two items need some explanation. I liked to express myself sometimes in terms of humor and wit. Later, I grew to understand that some of my humor was a defense against letting others come too close to me, and I've worked to curtail inappropriate humor. Since high school, I've enjoyed looking at the stars at night. As I pondered the vastness between the farthest star in the last galaxy and myself, I've sensed something religious, optimistic, and even humorous. In these ways I had a bemused sense of the universe. And as a youth, I felt, or thought I felt, faintly enchanted vibrations and magical possibilities in my hometown. As a senior citizen writer, I still faintly feel them when I visit Endicott, eighty miles from my home in East Syracuse.

Dave's Pursuits ~ Army, Irish-Italian Marriage, IBM

Even though WWII and the Korean War were over by the time we left high school, the compulsory draft continued; the Vietnam War was not yet a factor. Dave was engaged to Donna Pero and working at IBM when he was drafted. He and his comrades drove tanks in the motorized cavalry, which replaced the horse cavalry, through the Mohave Desert of California in war games. I asked Dave about the positives and negatives of Army life years after his tour of duty.

"The band playing, the flags in the breeze, crisp uniforms and shined shoes, all the troops turning on cue – an Army parade was an adrenaline experience," he said, glad to reminisce. "And I met some memorable guys, such as Hank, in the tank corps. But obeying some orders was challenging for me. Some sergeants were too authoritarian for peacetime."

In 1957, Dave married Donna Pero, an American with Italian background. It seemed so natural in Endicott to have inter-ethnic marriages. Donna and her parents, Sam and Clara, shared their ethnic traditions with Dave, Mom, and Dad, and vice versa. Both families were enriched by the marriage and have kept in touch over the decades. Joyce and I recently attended a four-generation picnic of the Pero family in Endicott.

Donna's family featured spiedies. A spiedie was a series of marinated lamb cubes held together by a skewer and cooked over charcoal. A piece of Roma's bread was used to pull the lamb from the skewer into a sandwich. Outsiders might call this delicacy lamb kabob at their peril.

"Never order lamb kabob in an Endicott restaurant. You could get thrown out of a spiedie joint for unwisely ordering a kabob," Dave said to a visiting Army friend according to Donna.

"Spiedies, IBM products, and E-J shoes are the top products of Endicott; in that order," she added. Further contention seethed over which Mediterranean family brought spiedies to town.

"Camillo Iacovelli's family was not the first with spiedies," Clara told me, eliminating one competitor for the honor. Camillo was famous for spiedies served at his long-running restaurant in Endwell, east of Endicott.

"The Peros brought spiedies from Sicily," said Sam, without any doubt in his voice.

"No, my Greek relatives brought spiedies to Endicott," friend Christo later said.

I don't know who brought them to America. In my judgment, today's spiedie cooks seriously err by including vegetables on the skewer, and worse yet, by substituting chicken, or beef, or pork for classic lamb. I noticed in an international cookbook that spiedies were cited as a variation of lamb kabob from the ethnic families of Endicott, New York, but in my view the book got it reversed. Lamb kabob was a poor excuse for the inimitable Endicott spiedies.

Sam Pero grew prize tomatoes in his garden, and Clara canned over a hundred jars of sauce to last a year. When Dave's appetite dipstick was down a quart of sauce, he was glad to fill up again at Clara's table. He enjoyed the many Italian dishes from her kitchen, and I'll never forget his story of a surprise gourmet treat. Donna dropped hints that something special was scheduled for Sunday dinner at the Pero home. After the antipasto and pasta courses, Donna set a huge covered dish with a distinct odor before Dave, and she dramatically took off the cover to reveal a steaming sheep's head. Dave was aghast at this specialty only for those with the acquired taste. He ran to the back porch to catch his breath and then politely declined the entree. Whenever Dave told the story, he stressed those animal eyes staring up at him through the odd-smelling steam. I must've heard Dave tell that story a dozen times.

"Were the eyes of the sheep like big marbles from a kid's game?" I asked, after he retold the story in late life.

"No, not quite."

"Were they like those of a horse?"

"No, not that big."

"Were they like the eyes of a doe?"

"No, not that soulful."

"Were they like those of an eagle?" I suggested, grasping for straws.

"No, too fierce."

"What then?" I asked, running out of comparisons.

"I've got it. The eyes staring up at me through the steam were like those of a hoot owl with cataracts," he said, nailing down the description to his satisfaction once and for all.

Dave advanced in his career at IBM where perceptions were important. Like Dad before him, he dutifully donned the IBM uniform of white shirt and modest tie. I don't remember when IBM first allowed colored dress shirts, but after decades of white shirts, top management finally permitted a more flexible range of colored shirts to go with conservative ties. In those days of comprehensive social change, the 1960s and 1970s, a famous folk song celebrated that "the times, they are a-changin'."

Seminary ~ The Rock

After discussion and reflection, I chose to enter the seminary at eighteen to study for the priesthood. I had the support of my family. Coming from an Irish-American-Catholic-Democratic-Northern family, I soon learned that my background was identical to that of many classmates. Other students counterbalanced and enriched variations on the theme; some were Italian-American-Catholic-Democratic-Northern, German etc., Hispanic etc., Polish etc. However, I guessed that by the middle of the 1950s, some parents of my classmates might have become Republicans as traditional voting blocks slowly weakened. As time went on, I found it to be clear as Waterford crystal that all of us were products of the immigrant model of church with its strengths and weaknesses.

If I asked twenty active or inactive priests today about their memories of seminary life, I would get twenty different views. Some would recall mostly positive elements, others would remember mostly negatives, and the moderates would remember a mix of memories. I've been blessed and cursed with a moderate mind. Because scholarly and critical books are available about seminary programs of philosophy, theology, and spirituality, I prefer to share mostly casual and light memories from the middle 1950s to the early '60s.

It didn't help that the red sandstone St. Bernard's Seminary in Rochester, New York was widely called "The Rock" for its strict discipline. It was like a benevolent penal colony for over 200 students. The lights came on at 5:30 a.m. and went out at 9:45 p.m. We didn't wear striped uniforms, but donned cassocks on grounds, except for sports. The food was institutional, and nobody was able to identify the contents of "porkball," a regular feature. I playfully concluded that my years at The Rock prompted me to like prison movies such as *The Shawshank Redemption* and *Papillon*.

Emphasis was on conformity and endurance. But we could walk away at any time, and some did. Most of us were of third- or fourth- or fifth-generation immigrant stock. Starry-eyed and intellectually bright, we had emotional growth and maturity yet to achieve, if not in the seminary, then in our years of priestly service as frank writers have recently pointed out. We came to the seminary with vague, idealistic notions of the calling to serve in the clergy, but we had eight years to discern whether the realistic demands of parish priesthood and the challenging requirement of mandatory celibacy were for us. And the seminary faculty supervised us. As we'll see in the next chapter, I served as parish priest for sixteen years and then resigned and married Joyce.

Sports were fun and one way to sublimate healthy bodily energy. One handballer we called "Killer (Jim) Kane" for his non-returnable kill shot. Strong players from the Syracuse Parochial League, such as Frank Woolever and Jack McCrea, enhanced our basketball games. We played hockey, and Bob Lavelle bumped many of us into near oblivion. Jerry Beirne introduced the non-contact game of cribbage for rainy day competition.

Softball was also a popular sport, and when I thought about it an extended memory came to me. I was minutes late for a game, and so I had to umpire. When "Orangie" hit a gargantuan blast, I took my position near third base. With one arm pointing toward home plate and the other arm lined up with an imaginary foul line along left field, I waited and waited for the ball, powered by the bat of mighty Orangie and the prevailing wind, to land.

"Foul ball!" I shouted gesturing dramatically, like Ron Luciano, famous and beloved umpire from Endicott. Orangie was soon in my face and shouting, "Fair ball . . . no foul . . . clearly fair."

"Foul ball!" I said, wiping from my face the unintended fine spittle spray of his wrath.

"Tu sicut vespertilio caecus," he said, lapsing into the Latin for "You're blind as a bat."

In the grand tradition of authoritarian umps, I didn't budge. "Play ball!" I shouted, in effect, changing the subject. To my surprise, Orangie and both teams immediately resumed the game.

Years later, I saw a gigantic umpire nullify an over-the-fence homer of a small Little Leaguer. The boy allegedly and inadvertently stepped on the line of the batter's box in hitting his home run. "Close enough," I said to myself while watching the disappointed lad, and the memory of Orangie's blast bubbled up in my mind to accuse me. By then, I had years of experience in helping others in pastoral ministry and realized that close enough was the norm for most people. I'd long concluded that divine justice and divine mercy are based on close enough. So let the official record now show that I erred by inches and that Orangie's wind-driven, Homeric homer of at least 350-plus feet is hereby considered the longest home run ever hit at The Rock in its long history of ferocious and testosterone-driven athletics.

Walking around the grounds one June, I noticed that Ray fell behind our group. I waited for him to catch up and saw that he was hobbling on the sides of his shoes.

"What's wrong, Ray?"

"My shoes have holes in the soles. I'm trying to make them last a few more days till we go home for the summer."

We chatted about summer jobs. He had outdoor work lined up again near his Syracuse home, and I was eager to work at IBM-Endicott again – this time as a landscaper. I told him that at IBM I had run a printing press, helped in electro-magnetic etching, and tracked records in an office. Summer jobs gave us needed cash and were good opportunities to experience different workplaces and interact with working men and women. As we neared Philosophy Hall, Ray hobbled to a trash can where year-end junk overflowed. He slipped out of his shoes and into some pitiful discards. "Fit just right," he said, without any sense of self-consciousness.

I sensed vaguely then and know clearly now that something significant had happened in that casual switching of shoes. Over the years I've thought of that scene and concluded that I had witnessed a friend taking seriously the gospels of Jesus about detachment from things. He went on to become Father Ray McVey, a social activist and pacifist priest whom many admired, but few were able to imitate in his total commitment to serve the urban poor and 125 homeless men with serious alcohol problems in a country setting at Unity Acres, north of Syracuse.

Some of our textbooks were in Latin, but not in classical Latin. Church Latin followed the English word order and wasn't difficult to read. I tried to remember the Latin definition of Philosophy, and I hope that I got it right: "Philosophia est scientia omnium cognoscibiliorum per ultimas causas." My translation: "Philosophy is the science of all things knowable through their ultimate causes." This was a tall order.

After four years of seminary study, we received a B.A. degree, recognized by New York State, in liberal arts with a major in Philosophy and went on to four years of Theology. We weren't trained as literal fundamentalists of the Bible, but as careful and patient students of the word of God. We learned that the Bible was not to be read superficially and casually like a newspaper. To interpret a given passage of the Bible, we had to understand the cultural history of Biblical times, the literary forms of those days, and the intention or purpose of the author (Job or Luke). Then we could begin to find the religious truth inspired by God in a given Bible passage.

I've long felt that thanks were due to Catholic, Protestant, and Jewish scholars for their careful, methodical efforts to break open the religious truths of the Bible. And I've realized how much intolerance, violence, and war flowed from religious forms of extreme fundamentalism. Our six years of church history wisely covered examples of fanatical Christian (Catholic included), Jewish, and Muslim extremism so that we might learn from the past. Any religion, not tempered by balance and scholarship, can be twisted into justifications for extremism and violence, and here's the tragic kicker – all done in God's name. All religions of "A Book," such as Judaism, Christianity, and Islam need balanced scholars to assist in careful interpretations.

Father Robert McNamara taught our history courses and Christian art from the catacombs to religious works of Salvador Dali and other moderns. In contrast to the discipline in his church history courses, he tolerated talking and horsing around during the occasional evening slide shows and lectures on Christian art. Slides of a handball match would be placed in with the works of El Greco or Raphael by one of the students. Despite being rowdies of the immigrant church, most of us somehow came to appreciate art. I was grateful later for his efforts to add some refinement to us.

The Power of Michelangelo ~ Model of Church

In a recent tour stop in Rome, Joyce and I visited the Vatican Museum, Sistine Chapel, and St. Peter's Basilica. Busloads of tourists from various countries followed intrepid guides with their color-coded flags held high. Hundreds of us were herded into the Sistine Chapel to view the overpowering fresco paintings by Michelangelo on the ceiling and walls. We were packed together, rubbing elbows and other body parts, sweaty and irritable. The constant flow of people through the chapel occasioned low murmuring and ooohing. As we sat along the wall, I thought back to Fr. McNamara's slides of the Sistine Chapel. Now over forty years later, I was thankful for the opportunity to see the originals. I later shared with Joyce how far I'd come since I'd been one of the rowdies during church art sessions.

In those minutes below and before the original works of Michelangelo, I also sensed that I was seeing a positive model of church. Like international tourists moving through the crowded chapel, the church was a people of God with members of different languages, races, and cultures on a journey through life together. Michelangelo with his riot of colors and human bodies – some clothed, some naked, and others clothed for centuries by Vatican prudes but now naked again after recent restoration of the frescos to their original state – told stories of the people of God.

Michelangelo's depictions of Bible stories were not sanitized, but earthy and full of human imperfections. The church, as people of God on a journey, was to me richer, more imperfect, and more human than authoritarian models of church.

I didn't think these thoughts all at once, but after we were home again the experience of the Sistine Chapel kept surfacing in my memory and nagging me until I wrote about it.

St. Bernard's Institute, with its new name, moved across the city to the ecumenical campus of Colgate Rochester Divinity School, Crozer (not Crozier) Theological Seminary, and Bexley Hall, where I presumed student life and curriculum are much different. Some women now teach and take Catholic seminary courses. I don't know whatever happened to the original buildings. Are they condos, maybe named "The Rock Gardens," for boomers and gen-Xers? Or nursing homes for the WWII generation? Or minimum-security facilities for minor offenders? If the latter, not many renovations would've been required with the already cell-like single rooms of old.

Grateful for Bittersweet and Alloyed Times

I belonged to the class of 1962, and I'd like to rank it a vintage year. Most of us were twenty-five or so at the time of ordination. After reviewing my years at The Rock, I evaluated them, without cheap shots and with my moderate mind, as not the best of times, as not the worst of times, but as mixed, bittersweet, and alloyed times. I've been grateful for the camaraderie that enriched and supported me in seminary life, later in pastoral service, and even in the present.

I've continued to value in particular three countercultural gospel lessons of Jesus that we learned in the seminary: detachment from things; the ideal to serve rather than to be served; and forgiveness of enemies, which, I believe, should be extended today to forgiveness of crippling debts of third world countries by America and other wealthy and developed nations. Activist Bono of the musical group U2 and others, such as Pope John Paul II, urge this debt forgiveness. These three Bible ideals challenged us as young Catholic priests to live, teach, and preach in countercultural opposition to the consumer society, in opposition to basic human selfishness, and in opposition to the all too human tendency to seek revenge and withhold forgiveness of enemies and debts. My classmates and I may not have always preached and practiced these ideals, but we left St. Bernard's Seminary fully understanding them. In those mostly conservative times just prior to Vatican Council II, we may not have considered ourselves as countercultural and non-violent agents of the revolutionary good news of Jesus, but looking back, I believe that we were.

Dave and I gave male representation to the fifth generation until Donna, and later Anne and Joyce, brought some feminine counterbalance. Two nieces bring with them more feminine changes in the next generation, and in the next chapter we'll see how our family's northern tradition was shattered, surprisingly and also permanently.

"A photo showed Dave and me in almost matching cowboy suits in 1940 – we looked like tiny versions of Roy Rogers and Gene Autry." Dave, Dad, and Jim, left to right.

"We were seasoned veterans of the home front...relieved that WWII was finally over." Jim, left, and Dave, 1945.

● **Jim Cuddy** of St. Ambrose appears to be readying the ball for a swallowing act in last night's game against St. Patrick's at the Endicott school gym. Instead, Jim was driving in for a layup shot with an unidentified St. Pat's player making a losing effort in attempting to stop him.

"There was a two-generation photo from the paper; I was shooting and Dad was in the bleachers behind me." Dad with glasses to right of ball, 1954.

"In 1957, Dave married Donna Pero, an American with Italian background. It seemed so natural in Endicott to have inter-ethnic marriages."

"In those mostly conservative times just prior to Vatican Council II, we may not have considered ourselves as countercultural and non-violent agents of the revolutionary good news of Jesus, but looking back, I believe that we were." 1962.

Chapter Six

Sixth Generation:
Family North & South Generation, 1959

*"If you're smart and keep your eyes and ears open,
you'll hear the stories of people who've survived
the unimaginable — who've persevered and endured,
despite the loss of loved ones, despite sickness, divorce,
bankruptcy, addiction, you name it."*

*Maria Shriver, Ten Things I Wish I'd Known —
Before I Went Out into the Real World*

Sixth Generation: Two Nieces

Becky Cuddy   Carolyn Cuddy
Born in 1959   Born in 1961

Feminine Style

As soon as Donna's labor alarm sounded, I joined more than ten family members noisily milling around the maternity waiting room. A nurse came out and said, "Why don't some of you go home? Nothing will happen for a while." Becky Cuddy, daughter of Dave and Donna Pero Cuddy, was born on August 24, 1959. Two years later, Carolyn Cuddy was born on April 21, 1961, and she also received an enthusiastic welcome by the family. Becky and Carolyn represented the sixth generation with feminine style.

One day Becky, age three or four, and I were on a walk around the block. Halfway around, she looked back a few times. Three-quarters around she began to have misgivings and turned back toward her home. I patiently tried to explain that we could go forward and arrive home sooner, but she wanted to retrace our steps. When she pointed back, I pointed forward, and we kept going. After reaching the 90% point where her house was almost in sight, she sat down on the sidewalk in impish protest, so I sat down. It became a game of generational wills.

"I can beat him. What's an uncle anyhow?" I imagined she was thinking behind her brow.

"I'm nine times older than this kid. I can outwit her," I thought. Before she tried more tactics, I scooped her up and ran the remaining distance. In seconds we were back on her porch with Donna. I then watched Becky's face for a while as she struggled to process the idea of walking in a big square.

I drew large squares to show her how we came home by always going forward. Then Donna and I witnessed the "Aha!" moment when she understood the basic idea that drove the discoverer Magellan to circumnavigate the earth.

"Okay!" she said. We walked around the block again to cement the lesson, and she kept pointing forward and pulling me to go faster. Upon reaching home, she danced a little jig to express her joy of learning.

When Carolyn was old enough to grasp the same idea, I arranged a special time to walk with her around the block. It was another struggle until she also finally grasped Magellan's concept. I was proud that I, as uncle, helped my nieces to acquire street smarts, and I was confident that they were savvy and hip – it was the '60s. They were girls who had been around the block and knew the meaning of it.

Some family stories are often retold because they capture the spirit of the lead character. Dave told this tale: "After Carolyn, at eight, learned about guardian angels at religious instruction, she told us about them in great detail. She was keen on the topic of angels, archangels, and the whole lot.

"'They watch over you, especially in time of need,' Carolyn told us, summing up the good services of guardian angels.

"'Well, what would you do if you were in need of help?' I asked. 'Let's say you were in some kind of danger.'

"'I guess,' Carolyn said, after a long pause, 'I'd call 911.'"

Moving South ~ Shattering a Tradition

Leaving hometown for a job advancement was a trend in America, and upwardly mobile professionals were moving south and west in the 1960s and subsequent decades. Dave and Donna shocked the family when they decided to move to North Carolina in 1965. Dave had a solid opportunity to advance with IBM by transferring from Endicott. They broke an unwritten rule that family members should live and die in Endicott with extended family nearby. Mom and Dad, as well as Sam and Clara, never fully got over Dave and Donna's move to the south. I had mixed feelings. Although I realized that I would miss them and their children, I supported their decision, even though it smashed one of the four traditions of our family – we were Northerners.

In their new home, in Raleigh, North Carolina, Dave and Donna hosted northern visitors of the Cuddy and Pero families over the years. Becky and Carolyn developed into lovely southern young women with delightful accents. Dave and Donna eventually lived longer in the south than in the north and definitely considered themselves southerners. This move permanently divided our family into the northern branch and the southern branch, just as the Mason-Dixon line demarcated the north and south in Civil War days.

Becky and Carolyn brought joy, vitality, and feminine strength to our family. We watched them grow, not only in our visits to their southern home, but also on their return visits to Endicott. I vividly recalled a Christmas season with Becky, Carolyn, and parents visiting in Endicott. I bought ice skates for the girls, and they opened these presents a few days early. I had dug out my old hockey skates, and we went skating at an outdoor rink in a former E-J park. The southern girls had a lively time learning to ice skate. When I'm now with Becky's children, Caroline and Carter of the seventh generation, I sometimes look up and see in my mind's eye Becky and Carolyn on skates. "How did one generation pass so quickly?" I ask myself.

Dave ~ Police Captain and Defender

Our family was definitely an IBM family. Dad had worked thirty-three years for IBM in Endicott, and Dave was with IBM even longer, mostly in North Carolina. IBM attracted and cultivated driven, team-playing employees, and the IBM culture and work ethic were legendary. Both Dad and Dave worked considerable overtime. Dad's overtime challenges came especially during WWII, and Dave's throughout his IBM career.

When Dave was working as an IBM manager in personnel, I asked him to describe his work. "I'm like Captain Frank Furillo, played by Daniel Travanti, on the TV police drama *Hill Street Blues*," he said. "I see Furillo as a personnel manager rather than a police captain." I partially understood and watched that program for several weeks with his comments in mind until I fully grasped his work.

"Now in my personnel work I'm like a defense attorney," Dave said, responding to my question about his career years later.

"Frazzled managers come to me and want to fire employees today, now, before closing. I say, 'Whoa, no one is fired until we follow IBM policies and procedures.'" Some employees received an acquittal with Dave acting in their defense. Continuing his boyhood reputation of cutting pies evenly, he strove for a fair process for all.

Dave advanced steadily at IBM. I saw a videotape of him as one of the speakers at his friend's retirement dinner and enjoyed his humor and cleverness. Because he lived more than 600 miles away, I didn't know many facets of Dave's professional life. It was the first time I saw him as a public speaker. Dave also had a passion for the TV game show *Jeopardy!* With his wide reading and remarkable memory, he became a formidable *Jeopardy* player with his family, friends, and IBM colleagues. He sometimes conceded Single *Jeopardy* to his opponents and tried to catch them in Double *Jeopardy*.

Marriages, divorces, and remarriages are in the stories of most families. Divorces challenge other family members to grow and widen their non-judgmental and inclusive skills. Dave and Donna divorced when Becky and Carolyn were in high school and junior high. Dave spent as much time as he could with the girls who preferred to go separately to dinner and on outings with him. Family life goes on after divorce. In watching many families deal with the complexities of divorce, I've noticed that children show considerable resilience as long as they experience continuity in being loved and feeling loved.

Years later Dave married Anne Prince, a native of North Carolina and an IBM manager. She deepened Dave's conversion to the south. Dave and Anne enjoyed travel and visited Camp Irwin in the Mohave Desert to view his Army haunts. They also traveled to many foreign countries. In Ireland's County Mayo, Dave and Anne stayed at luxurious Ashford Castle. They were the first family members to stay in a castle since the ancient chieftains of the MacGillacudda clan ruled The Reeks and surrounding glens of County Kerry. In their tour of Kerry, they drove over a rugged mountain pass miles south of The Reeks and raved about the mountain views. In addition, Anne's passion for opera increased Dave's enjoyment of great operas and arias.

Anne also arranged positive three-generation reunions for our family in Ottawa, Philadelphia, Boston, Disney World, Baltimore, and the North Carolina beach. Mom and Aunt Jule were able, despite their advanced ages, to attend most of these reunions. In addition, Anne and Donna got along well.

"Am I the only man in North Carolina whose wife and former wife attend the same parties?" Dave said to me, rolling his eyes and then pointing to Anne and Donna, engaged in a chat at an inclusive family party.

Becky and Carolyn had only one aunt and one uncle, Linda Pero and me. She gave much love and support to the girls throughout the years. Linda skillfully taught public school children with special developmental needs and inspired Becky and Carolyn to dream of teaching careers. Both girls spent hours at play, teaching dolls and imaginary pupils. Becky, in time, became a dedicated teacher, but Carolyn didn't have a chance to follow her dreams.

Trauma of a Lost Young Life

The death of a young daughter or son is one of life's deepest sorrows. Niece Carolyn died in a car accident near her home on April 5, 1980. She was eighteen and a first year student at East Carolina University. In her death, our family suffered one of the greatest traumas to its spirit in six generations. Dave never completely got over her death. In time, Dave and Anne helped other parents who were dealing with the death of a son or daughter.

Mom was visiting Joyce and me when we received Dave's telephone call about Carolyn's death. First I tried to console Dave, Mom, and Joyce. Then I made reservations, in a cool and detached way, for us to fly to Raleigh, North Carolina for the funeral. I had often dealt with death in parish ministry and kept myself insulated by intellectualizing. But I soon needed to sit on the sofa where the emotional impact of Carolyn's death struck me like a tornado out of nowhere. From a primal source inside me I uttered a series of groans. If I, an uncle living over 600 miles away, felt her death on such a visceral level, how did her parents, stepmother, and sister deal with her death? Some feelings may be too intense to describe.

Carolyn died near Easter, and we drew strength from Christ's victory over death, but not in a simplistic or superficial way. In my view, grief is a complex process to be worked through over time. Dave, Anne, Donna, and Becky struggled with the process of grief in North Carolina with the help of friends. Carolyn's maternal grandparents, Sam and Clara Pero, Gram Veronica Cuddy, Aunt Linda Pero, Joyce, and I grieved and gave support from up north. Amy Tan, in *The Hundred Secret Senses*, gives an unusual insight into death: "I once thought love was supposed to be nothing but bliss. I now know it is also worry and grief, hope and trust. And believing in ghosts – that's believing that love never dies. If people we love die, then they are lost only to our ordinary senses. If we remember, we can find them anytime with our hundred secret senses." Carolyn, we'll always remember you.

The shadow of death eventually lifted, and our family focused on life again. Becky earned her first degree from North Carolina University, and in time, married Steve Parham, fellow graduate from NCU and a health insurance administrator. We celebrated these events in life-affirming ways; life meant more to us now. Becky and Steve, the remaining family representatives of the sixth generation, were vital for our family's future. They moved, as Steve rose in his career in health insurance management, to Los Angeles, Chicago, Chattanooga, Charlotte, Atlanta, and then Greensboro, North Carolina. The sixth generation has been on the move.

Parish Ministry ~ Lighthearted and Serious Stories

"Jim, tell us a story about being a Catholic priest," Becky said to me a few years before the above family trauma.

"What are your priest friends like?" Carolyn added. I paused a long time before selecting stories that would have meaning for them.

I now faced a similar challenge in this book. Others have written more formal books about parish ministry, but I wanted to share with the reader stories about priestly service that would harmonize with the tone of this book and the flow of generational stories. I preferred to share mostly lighthearted anecdotes, but I included some serious stories as well.

For me life was based on human relationships, and so I shaped relational stories into a casual composite or mosaic of priestly ministry in the 1960s and '70s. I carefully chose stories involving a minister, rabbi, religious education director, pastor-storyteller, Army Chaplain, nine Korean babies, a social activist priest, but I'm getting ahead of myself.

After joyful ordination in 1962, I served as Associate Pastor in parishes not far from Endicott for sixteen years. I concluded from my years of pastoral experience that parish ministry, sometimes routine and sometimes dramatic, was the most challenging type of priestly service because it covered the spectrum from new life to death, from infant baptism to funeral and burial rites. Parish priests were unusual in many ways; we were spiritual general practitioners in an age of specialists, and we still made house calls.

When I served as Associate Pastor in Vestal, New York, in the late '60s, I volunteered for an inter-religious pilot program. A team consisting of an Episcopalian priest, a religious education director, a rabbi, and a Catholic priest taught an elective course about religion and values to public school students inside Vestal Public High School. The U.S. Supreme Court has allowed teaching *about* religion and values in the public schools, but not the teaching *of* denominational religion and values. Team members strove to be objective in class presentations.

The team leaders were The Reverend W. Kilmer Sites, Pastor of St. Andrew's Episcopal Church, and Barbara C. Blossom, Education Director for the same church. They did most of the work on the course and were the authors of the eventual textbook, *Ethics In Perspective and Practice*. They also offered training programs for public school teachers. Rabbi Elihu Schagrin of Temple Concord in Binghamton wrote the parts on Jewish ethics for the textbook and taught those units. I wrote the parts on Catholic ethics for the textbook and covered those topics in class. The students who chose this elective course joined in discussions and asked challenging questions after they became comfortable with us.

The Second Vatican Council in one of its documents encouraged ecumenism, which meant dialogue and action among Catholic, Orthodox, and Protestant Christians. In another document, the Council encouraged inter-religious dialogue and action between Catholics and Jews, and also among Catholics and those of non-Biblical religions. Against this background, I found it rewarding and exciting to work side-by-side with Protestant and Jewish colleagues in practical ways. Barbara Blossom and I have kept in touch for over thirty years.

In 1971, the National Federation of Priests' Councils (these councils of priests advised bishops in dioceses after Vatican Council II) held its convention in Baltimore, and I was one of two delegates from the Priests' Council of the Syracuse Diocese. I was fortunate enough to attend the following year as well, but in Denver. We voted on many resolutions for helping the poor, fostering reform and renewal, and implementing the decrees of the Second Vatican Council. On a resolution encouraging optional celibacy for priests, the older delegate from the Syracuse diocese and I voted on opposite sides. He opposed the resolution, and I supported the proposed change. Our split vote reflected our personal views and represented the divided positions of the priests back home. The vote was dramatic, and the resolution that advised optional celibacy passed, but the vote was only a straw poll. We knew that we weren't legislating changes and celibacy is still not optional, but we were reflecting the changing attitudes and priorities of many priests in America in 1971. Years later I noticed that vote in a footnote of a scholarly book.

My vote in Baltimore for optional celibacy for priests was a theoretical vote for me. I had no personal stake in such a reform. I merely held the opinion that optional celibacy would mean more people would want to become priests. In my opinion, choosing celibacy is better than accepting celibacy mandated by church disciplinary law. Priests should have the choice to marry. Later, I describe how celibacy became a personal issue for me in 1978 when I had to decide between my head and my heart, between remaining in celibate parish ministry or resigning to marry Joyce.

The Binghamton paper interviewed both delegates on our return. A very conservative parishioner, I'll call him Mr. X, reacted to the newspaper article by telephoning me and strongly opposing reforms. He told me "to love the church or leave it." I welcomed the opportunity to share with him the context and meaning of the national convention in Baltimore. As I started to speak, he slammed down his phone.

A few Sundays later I noticed him sitting on the end of the pew about halfway down the center aisle. At the sign of peace I usually greeted the people on the aisle in a few front pews. This time I worked my way down more than a dozen pews toward the phone caller. I could see that he was beginning to fidget as I neared his pew. He had his hat in hand, and I was concerned that he might bolt for the door. At last, I positioned myself so that I blocked him from exiting the pew.

"Peace be with you, Mr. X," I said in a friendly way. He gave the reply and shook my extended hand. I recently pondered that simple exchange and felt that it symbolized what is needed in the Catholic Church today. Liberals, centrists/moderates, and conservatives need to at least co-exist and, even better, to get along with one another, and not just at the Sunday liturgy.

Ecumenical and interfaith work and the two national conventions were significant internal developments for me. I'd been living in a small upstate New York area for thirty-four years: growing up in Endicott, education in nearby Rochester, and parish service near Endicott. I had driven to California so I knew that our country and planet were vast, but I was provincial in my intellectual and professional life. These experiences weren't lighting bolts out of the blue sky, but rather mind-expanding and maturing events that gradually transformed me, and I've remembered and treasured them to the present day. I found that, once expanded, my mind never returned to its earlier narrower form, just as my religious practice, once internalized, didn't revert to mere external practice.

Monsignor Sheehan ~ The Church Storyteller

Monsignor Lawrence Sheehan, pastor of St. Thomas Aquinas parish in Binghamton, was a kind and dedicated type of priest that made Catholics proud, and I was happy to be an Associate Pastor with him. After the reforms of the Second Vatican Council, the late '60s and '70s were a time of great change, and a challenging and heady time to be alive in the Catholic Church. As an ecclesiastical seanachie, Monsignor Sheehan told many wonderful stories that preserved merry memories. His best story concerned an apology, and he changed the real names to fictional ones to protect privacy.

"Eighty years ago, three parish priests became mixed up in politics over a proposed new bridge in Binghamton. Feisty Father Donahue in a sermon opposed the bridge and insulted two priests, blood brothers, who were on the other side of the river and issue," Monsignor Sheehan began his story.

"'They both inherited long, pointy noses,' said Father Donahue. 'Well, just let Father John Ryan stand on the north side of the Susquehanna River, and Father Joseph Ryan stand on the south shore. Their noses would meet to span the river, and we wouldn't need another bridge.'

"The brothers took offense. The bishop, eighty miles away in Syracuse, demanded a public apology. Word was leaked, and some insisted that Father Donahue leaked it. Parishioners, plus many from other faiths, and a few non-believers – all expected high drama – wedged into the pews. Latecomers stood seven deep in the rear. As Father Donahue wove together Biblical themes of contrition in his sermon, a few pious types were weeping, but most were patient. They knew their man.

"'In conclusion,' Fr. Donahue said, and all leaned forward to catch his final words, 'at the request of the Bishop, I sincerely apologize to Father John Ryan and Father Joseph Ryan, grand priests one and all,' he paused for effect, 'even though we all know they both have noses that could pick a lock.' All tried not to laugh.

"'Bull's eye!' church trustee Fagan said, in an Irish whisper. Then the people broke into waves of laughter, but they said Father Donahue only smiled a coy smile. One pious fraud fainted and required smelling salts from the ushers. The bishop decided a second apology was too risky and dropped the matter." Monsignor Sheehan always convulsed with laughter at the end of his tale.

Many bridges spanned the Susquehanna in Binghamton, and I presume the bridge was built, perhaps partly in defiance of Father Donahue. As a strong pastor of the immigrant church, he may have been too powerful a force in the city. Sometimes when I cross a bridge there, this story bubbles up in my memory like champagne from the nearby Finger Lakes wineries. When I heard his apology story thirty years ago, I pledged to Monsignor Sheehan that I would someday write it down for the public record – a promise kept.

"Is it fact or fiction?" people always asked whenever I told this story.

"Monsignor Sheehan always claimed it was true," I said. "And I've held that it was too good a story not to be true."

Adventures of Father John, Army Chaplain

Father John Weyand and his family visited our family, and vice versa, throughout the years. Dad and Mom enjoyed stories of his adventures, and some tales about him became part of our family's lore. After a time in parish ministry, he served as Army Chaplain for over twenty years. I visited him at Army bases in or near Brooklyn, Savannah, Seattle, rural Maryland, and Washington DC, but I missed a visit to his base in the strange and isolated high desert southwest of Salt Lake City. I came to appreciate that his ministering to our soldiers in Vietnam, South Korea, and Germany and serving them and their families in various assignments in the U.S. were complex challenges. He was Captain and, in time, became Major.

Whenever I've lost valuables or become upset after I've been had, or conned, or flimflammed, I've remembered my favorite story about Chaplain John. For goings to and comings from bases overseas and throughout the United States, the Army diligently packed his gear and personal items in sturdy wooden crates. Sometimes crates were misplaced or stolen; twice his crates vanished, but John never let it bother him.

"Nobody is really free as a person until all of one's earthly possessions are gone twice," he explained to me in his usual understated way. A stick in the eye of materialism.

The next tale describes a civilian enterprise, not an Army one. Chaplain John and other soldiers signed up for training, during free time, to learn whether when going home on leave, they had the "right stuff" to bring infants-for-adoption on a commercial airplane from South Korea to New York City. A free plane ticket was the reward for each soldier willing to manage three babies in transit.

After a day of special childcare training, Chaplain John and two other soldiers agreed to the plan. Each soldier had extra seats. At the last minute, nine Korean social workers brought on board nine babies in safety seats, a load of pampers, and bottles of formula and then deplaned. Social workers had predicted from the experience of earlier flights that passengers at first would be annoyed or indignant over nine infants, but several eventually would offer to help. True to form, some bored and restless passengers on the long flight volunteered to assist with holding, feeding, burping, and changing the babies. When they finally arrived at a NYC airport, nine American social workers came on board and carried the infants to nine eagerly waiting adoptive couples.

To Chaplain John, adventures were the rule rather than the exception. After twenty-one years in the military, he spent eleven more as hospital chaplain and pastor. He retired from active ministry and married Gloria. Joyce and I are good friends with them and visit often.

Father McVey of Unity Acres

The autumn leaves were peaking the day I visited Father Ray McVey, a friend from my days in the seminary, at Unity Acres, a large unused county sanitarium that was purchased and refurbished by Ray and a large, dedicated team to serve about 125 homeless men with alcohol problems. It was located in the rural town of Orwell, north of Syracuse. I noticed that he wore his trademark uniform of work boots, green sweatshirt, and work pants. Ray and I visited so long that he invited me to stay over.

"This room ought to be fine," he said, after taking a key from a huge keyboard. "The regular resident is in the hospital." I saw that Ray had his bedroll on a wide shelf in his office for his own use. No springs. When I inspected my room, the linens were used, but the bed, happily for me, had springs. Instead of seeking fresh linens, I took a sleeping bag, stored in my car, put it on the bed and slept well.

"I trust that room worked out," Ray said at breakfast in the large dining room.

"Just fine," I answered. I respected Ray for not apologizing or making excuses for the quality of his accommodations. He lived in poor conditions with a community of Catholic Workers, volunteers, and residents and presumed everyone else would adjust. Driving back to my conventional rectory in Binghamton, I felt very middle-class, very middle-church, and very middle-aged.

Ray died and was buried at Unity Acres. When Joyce and I, with friends, recently visited his grave, I heard or thought I heard Ray's laughter. The project goes on, and donations are always needed to support this unique service program at Unity Acres, Box 153, Orwell, NY 13426.

When I visited, not long ago, with Fr. Ray's sister Betty, she showed me pictures and scrapbooks about him; he had died five years prior to our talk. She noted that one box for the albums had a *Survivor* logo for the brand of boots he wore throughout his years at Unity Acres. This triggered her memory to recall a story about Ray's footwear.

"'Once we noticed that one of Ray's boots had a big hole in the sole. We bought him a pair of *Survivor* boots and gave them to him in the box as he was returning to Unity Acres,' she said, enjoying the role of storyteller. 'The next time we saw him, he was wearing those old boots again.'

"'What happened to your new boots?' I asked Ray.

'Oh, I gave them to someone who needed them,' Ray responded. After that, whenever Ray wore out his boots, I discarded them and insisted he wear the new replacement boots we bought for him back to Unity Acres."

"A holy soul with a holey sole," I said, trying to get the right summary of his life of service. I borrowed her copy of the captivating book: *No Problem, The Story of Father Raymond McVey and Unity Acres, A Catholic Worker House* (1998). This book caught the essence of Fr. Ray, his radical commitment to the Sermon on the Mount by Jesus, his service mentality and his humor. It also told of many other key players on the team and the Catholic Worker spirit.

A mosaic of priestly service in the 1960s and '70s could be crafted and assembled in many ways by different priests, writers, and artists. These stories formed the pieces of my artwork. Like an artist, I reviewed my mosaic looking at it from one side and another and pondering it in varying light. I've tried to capture the lighthearted side of service, adding pieces for balance, and I hope that I've accomplished that.

Sister Joyce, Miss LaCasse, Mrs. Cuddy

I first met Joyce LaCasse in Binghamton. She served as a Sister of St. Joseph. After a while she felt it was time to move on; she left religious life, moved to the Syracuse area, and switched from parochial to public elementary school teaching. Joyce, like most former sisters, left convent life for several reasons.

"After all the changes of Vatican Council II, the divide between sisters and lay people was less dramatic. I felt drawn to continue my Christian life as a laywoman," she said to me.

Joyce recently attended a delightful reunion, held in the Catskills, of all sisters and former sisters from her class of 1958. Out of thirty-six members, nine have remained in the order, and twenty-seven have pursued other careers, mostly in service professions. Many have married. The Sisters of St. Joseph, with the Motherhouse in Latham, NY, have made special efforts to include Joyce and all former sisters in their mailings, gatherings, and special events.

After Joyce left the convent, our acquaintanceship was later renewed, grew into friendship, and that developed into love.

In 1978, after sixteen years of parish ministry, I came to a crossroads. For me the difficult decision was either to resign from the priesthood and marry or remain in celibate service. If I could have married Joyce and remained an active priest, I would have, but that was not a choice I was given. After time for prayer, counseling, and leave of absence, I resigned from the active priesthood and asked Joyce to be my wife. She accepted, and we've grown in love and sharing as the years passed. We recently renewed our marriage covenant in the company of friends on our twenty-fifth wedding anniversary.

We didn't see marriage as a magical solution to life's abiding challenges. We had the maturity to realize that marriage was a challenge in its own right. Joyce's approach to work, life, and marriage was prose and nonfiction, and mine was complementary poetry and fiction. Mom – Dad had died – Dave, Anne, and nieces Becky and Carolyn welcomed Joyce into our small family, and Joyce and Mom became friends.

Joyce was a spirited, organized, and no-nonsense teacher for thirty-two years, mainly in fifth grade, and she won an award for excellence in teaching. Former students have sought her out to thank her for guiding them and meeting their educational and personal needs. Also parents of some of her students have thanked Joyce for instilling study habits that enabled their future success. We've met her former students in malls and other places, and they've enjoyed reminiscing about the good old days of fifth grade.

Joyce's parents and family accepted me into their large family of French-Canadian-Americans. Her father "Frenchy" had been a lumberjack who worked both sides of the Quebec-Maine border. He married Irene Marois, and Joyce has a lovely newspaper notice of their wedding in 1927. They settled in the French-Canadian-American village of Cohoes, near Albany, NY. Joyce's family of eight brothers and sisters has staged huge reunions that we've enjoyed. Joyce and I visited Montreal, Quebec City, and Paris and appreciated her family roots.

Mid-life Career Change ~ Human Services

In mid-life, I began, with a degree in Philosophy, a new career in human services. I joined the War on Poverty, begun earlier by President Lyndon Johnson. I became a planner and grant writer at Cayuga County Action Program, twenty-five miles west of Syracuse. Executive Director Gloria Griffin, an African-American, was a champion of minorities and the poor, and I learned much from this strong advocate and community leader. I also gained wisdom from many younger and hipper colleagues in the war on poverty. When I represented our agency on the Board of Emergency Medical Services, I was mistaken a few times for Judge James G. Cuddy. There were many Cuddys in the Auburn, NY phone book, but none were relatives.

In the course of my work, Joyce and I joined in a March on Washington, DC to urge continued funding of programs for the poor. Labor unions sent many members to march with us. Our chartered bus from Auburn drove all night, and the sun came up as we drove along the Beltway around Washington, which was crowded with hundreds of buses filled with marchers. Advance planning sheets even told us what Beltway exit to use to avoid bus bottlenecks. The march was effective, and funding for the poor continued. I wish every American could march on Washington in support of some worthy cause, or civic issue, or conscience concern, at least once.

My last eleven years before retirement I spent at Loretto in Syracuse. This huge organization had on its campus a thirteen-story nursing home, clinic, home for those with Alzheimer's disease, and a twenty-two-story high-rise for senior housing. Other Loretto senior services were scattered throughout the county. I worked as an administrator for four group homes for seniors with psychiatric needs or developmental disabilities. The homes were located in the community. Like a choreographer, I was responsible to make sure the staff was dancing together to the same music. With support from untiring and professional colleague Karen O'Hara, energetic Dan Engelhardt, versatile Dave Mooney, committed hands-on workers, day programs, psychiatric supervision, and modern medications, our elderly residents thrived in the home-like atmosphere of group homes. The proof of our team's service was found in the positive feedback from state inspectors and from those we served.

Neighbor Joe Lovely faithfully visited his wife Ellie at Loretto Nursing Home, and Joyce and I, in retirement, sometimes accompanied him. Like a retired fire horse reacting to the clang of the distant fire bell, I remember my Loretto days whenever I returned to campus. In time, Joe became a resident in the same nursing home, and Joyce and I visit them regularly.

Joe and Ellie have eight grandchildren; the six younger ones have enriched Joyce and me. In support of them, we attended a baptism, piano recitals, plays, a moving naturalization ceremony, and we took them on successful fishing expeditions for bluegills. Some of these children have called us "fairy grandparents." As fairy grandfather, I've included this story about their real grandfather Joe. I've told this story a few times, and it's become grafted onto our family yarns.

Joe, a well-known Rhode Island chef, was reluctant to write down and share his famous recipes. Several years ago, he was in the hospital at death's door. The parish priest had given Joe the anointing of the sick a few times, but this time he was in serious jeopardy, and the family said their good-byes. Silence fell over the family gathered around the bed.

"There's one last thing, Joe!" sister Jan said, with her pen and paper ready. "Don't die on us now. We need the exact recipe for your famous fish chowder before it's too late." Family laughter followed her statement. "I'm serious. After all these years we still don't have the details."

"Don't forget the . . ." Joe whispered.

"Don't forget what, Joe?"

"Don't forget the . . ."

"What Joe? Don't forget what? For God's sake, Joe," she said exasperatedly.

"The bay leaves, zz, zzzz, zzzzzz."

Joe outwitted them once again. He made a mysterious recovery and later resumed making fish chowder at his retirement home next-door to Joyce and me. To this day, his family hasn't yet inherited the secret recipe. Joe's family members, just like my relatives, were able to laugh even in the face of death or near-death because they believed death was not the end of everything. They expected to see one another again in the afterlife.

As the 1990s dawned, our family began to hope for the arrival of the seventh generation. Nature has a plan. Just when an extended family settles into predictable and routine living, things are turned upside down by the advent of a new generation. John Cuddy, Dave Cuddy, and Becky Cuddy Parham were firstborns of the fourth, fifth, and sixth generations. And now here comes Caroline Parham, first one of the seventh generation out of the gate.

"Carolyn, we'll always remember you."
High School Graduate, 1979.

"Becky...married Steve Parham, fellow graduate from NCU
and a health insurance administrator."
Left to right: Dave, Mom, Becky, Steve, and Anne, 1983.

"Years later Dave married Anne Prince, a native of North Carolina and an IBM manager." 1979.

"Joyce's approach to work, life, and marriage was prose and nonfiction, and mine was complementary poetry and fiction." Jim and Joyce at their wedding celebration, 1978.

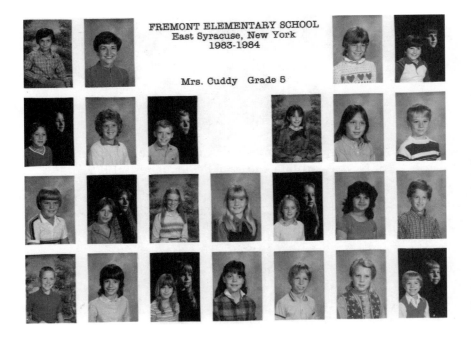

FREMONT ELEMENTARY SCHOOL
East Syracuse, New York
1983-1984

Mrs. Cuddy   Grade 5

"Joyce was a spirited, organized, and no-nonsense teacher for thirty-two years, mainly in the fifth grade, and she won an award for excellence in teaching." 1984.

Chapter Seven

Seventh Generation: Computer Generation, 1991

"We deplore, and hold ourselves morally bound, to protest and resist, in church and society, all actions, customs, laws and structures that treat women or men as less than fully human. We pledge ourselves to carry forth the heritage of Biblical justice, which mandates that all persons share in right relationship with each other, with the cosmos, and with the Creator."

Excerpt from "The Madeleva Manifesto"
Signed by Sixteen Catholic Women, in 2000

Seventh Generation: Grandniece and Grandnephew

Caroline Elizabeth Parham   Stephen Carter Parham, Jr.
Born in 1991   Born in 1995

A typical conversation among senior citizens progresses to "quick-draw," the sudden reaching for the wallet, not to pay the lunch bill, but to show pictures of grandchildren. I quick-draw, but my pictures are of Grandniece Caroline and Grandnephew Carter. Of course, I boast they are the smartest and most attractive children on earth. It's crucial to win the draw, because the loser must patiently view pictures and listen to tall tales of soccer, tap dancing, computer skills, and report cards. By the time the loser gets to show photos and tell exaggerated stories, it's anticlimactic, and the winner becomes quickly disinterested. Seniors play for keeps.

Caroline and Carter ~ Pieces of Immortality

Grandniece Caroline Parham, daughter of Becky and Steve Parham, was born on May 23, 1991, in North Carolina, first child of the seventh generation. Grandnephew Carter Parham was born on June 27, 1995, in Georgia, first male in two generations. They've brought new vitality and hope to our family. One part of immortality is that we live on in future generations. Their births began a new generation, the seventh and latest, although I speculate about the eighth generation. I wrote a verse for Caroline's birth and also used it for Carter's. It gives a playful insight into the emergence of new life.

Be Nimble, Be Quick
New life is growing
And j
        u
          m
            p
              s from womb to Becky's arms
In the blink of a video camera, held steadily by Steve.

136

A "quick-draw" photo of three generations: Jim and Joyce Cuddy
(5th gen.), on ends, niece Becky Parham and Steve Parham
(6th gen.), center adults, Caroline and Carter Parham (7th gen.),
children, 1995.

The above three-generation photo captured the modern generations and was a companion picture to go with the four-generation photo of early ancestors in the first chapter. These two photographs, when set side by side, depict a chain of seven generations and concentrate the scope of our family saga in a visual way. Both pictures have special meaning for me.

Caroline and Carter are now thirteen and nine. They are already part of the computer generation at home and at school. When Joyce and I visited, we watched them on the computer and took them fishing, kite flying, swimming, and we occasionally baby-sat them. We read to them from classic children's books as well as from more recent works. Joyce and I are not grandparents, but we're learning our roles of grandaunt and granduncle. Because grandaunt and granduncle seemed uncomfortably close to pompous grandam and grand duke, we asked Caroline and Carter to call us Joyce and Jim, just as Joe Cawley told his grandchildren to call him Joe, three generations earlier.

Caroline has a lovely southern accent, and Carter called one barnyard animal a "piieegg."

"What's a piieegg?" I asked.

"You know, the oink-oink animal."

We've enjoyed watching developmental differences between girl and boy. I discovered that Caroline had over two dozen pairs of shoes and sneakers of every kind and Carter had many hats reflecting sports, trucking, and the army. This matched our experience. Joyce has lots of shoes and sneakers, and I have too many hats and caps, especially straw hats.

One day while reading the morning paper in the living room at Caroline and Carter's home, I noticed Caroline coming down the stairs for breakfast, but she didn't see me. When she reached a large cardboard barricade, keeping dog Max downstairs, she carefully removed it, stepped to room level, and then put it back. A few minutes later Carter came down in his cowboy suit, and not noticing me, kicked the barricade and sent it flying. He strode, like John Wayne, into the kitchen, while Max scampered up the stairs. This was not a scientific test from behind a two-way glass, but I did witness a significant scene that broke the code, in part, about gender differences.

At an early age Caroline and Carter learned from their mother about Christian service to others. Becky, a deacon in her moderate Southern Baptist Church, helped to settle a family with several children and one on the way. Having fled the war in Kosovo, the refugees lived in an apartment while church members repaired a church-owned house. Becky and her team have worked together to help these newcomers adjust. When Joyce and I first met the family members at a church supper, they insisted we come to their nearby home. Even though all of us had just eaten at church, they served chai tea and a snack. Reciprocal hospitality was important to them. Becky also modeled service by joining a team for a working visit to missions in South America. She was moved by the poverty and yet generosity of the natives.

Brother Dave's Passing ~ A Gaelic Farewell

Brother Dave, IBM retiree, died on October 11, 1997. Anne provided generous care for him especially in his final year. Some hold that we can't know the time of our death, but that we can have some limited input into the circumstances. If this is true, Dave died on his own terms, in bed, at home. He was his own man in life and in death.

Anne coordinated the funeral services and selected some of Dave's favorite classical music for the ceremony. I wrote a brief family history for the service, which included these words: "I quoted a line of poetry by G. K. Chesterton to Dave years ago, and he repeated it to me many times, 'The great Gaels of Ireland are men that God made mad, for all their wars are merry and all their songs are sad.' By different routes, Dave and I were able to realize the strengths and weaknesses inherent in our shared ethnic origin." Dave's friend and IBM retiree, Pete Mutchler, gave a eulogy balanced with humor. The soft music of "Danny Boy" ended the service.

Later that day, Anne, Becky, Joyce, and I took Dave's cremated remains to the cemetery for the burial service. The urn was still warm from his ashes, which triggered our laughter.

"Should we be laughing?" I said.

"Dave would think it was funny," Joyce said. We drove to the cemetery with intermittent laughter as each held the warm urn for a while. I heard or thought I heard Dave's faint laughter while I cradled the urn. His remains now rest close to the grave of his daughter Carolyn. There are no words to take away the pain of death in the family. We miss both of them.

Fishing Gene Activated

After the funeral, I brought Dad's stuffed fish from Dave's garage in my hand luggage to its native upstate New York. The airport security lady wanted more information about the unusual silhouette on the X-ray screen.

"What's that odd thing in your bag?" she queried, returning my carryon.

"A fish." I opened the bag and surrendered it wrapped in a T-shirt.

"It doesn't smell fishy," she noted, sniffing it warily.

"No, a stuffed fish to put on the wall of my garage," I said, unwrapping the evidence. She carefully looked at it and with world-weariness waved me through.

In my middle and late years, I activated the fishing gene from Dad by ocean fishing off Nova Scotia, Long Island in New York, New Jersey, Florida, Oregon, Washington, and Ireland. I prefer going for bluefish at night out of Belmar, NJ, where the six-hour party boat returns about 1:30 a.m. Of late, younger guys have called me "Pops," and this stung more than turning sixty-five and going on Medicare. In the still of the night out at sea, I sometimes thought of Dad and wished that he could've experienced the thrill of fishing for blues when they were biting at the "Mud Hole," about twelve miles east of Belmar Inlet.

One full moon night in late May, the captain moved the party boat with about twenty customers from a weak spot and searched on his electronic fish-finder until he found blues below at the vast Mud Hole. The wind came up, the sea became choppy, the boat lurched, and then the bluefish went on a feeding frenzy.

"Fish on! Fish on! Fish on!" three customers yelled for the two mates to hoist their bluefish into the boat with long gaff hooks.

"Fish on! Fish on! Fish on!" a young couple and I shouted as we reeled in fighting blues.

Decks echoed with blues drumming their tails, mates were running back and forth with gaff hooks, a few fishers were untying crossed lines, and two seasick teens were heaving and retching over the side. The deck became as slick as butter from oily blues, fish blood, chunks of bunker bait, and a trail of vomit – another seasick case didn't make it to the rail.

The fish kept biting, but one by one we sat down to rest. A roughneck, proud of his big blue, tried to march around the lurching boat to show off his fish, but kept slipping on the oily deck.

"I love fishing at midnight!" he said and bayed at the moon. His comrades pounded their barrel chests and loudly chanted the same refrain. The young couple looked alarmed at their rowdiness.

"Sometimes bluefishing is a primitive experience," I told them. "Those good old Jersey guys are just blowing off steam. They would give you the last two life preservers in 'a perfect storm.'" As usual, I gave my fish to a willing family. Of course, I don't write about those nights when I catch few or even no blues.

After docking, I tiptoed into the motel room across the street to avoid waking Joyce. I stuffed my fishy-smelling clothes and hiking boots into a big plastic bag for washing later. In the shower I thought, "On productive nights, fishing for blues is not for the faint-of-heart, but Dad, a relentless fisherman, like Captain Ahab, would've enjoyed it as much as I do."

In a recent visit to our home, Caroline, Carter, and Becky went fishing with me. Using night crawlers, we caught an azure streak of bluegills, all of which we returned to the lake. The family tradition of fishing has been passed on, and I plan to hand on to Caroline or Carter my Dad's stuffed fish as an *heirloom* of sentimental value. The fish, having hung in Dad's attic, then in Dave's garage, and now in my garage, has emotional meaning, as did Corporal Dean's Civil War rifle.

Irish-American-Multiethnic Tradition Now

Flexibility in individuals and families fosters growth and development. Most families have struggled with tension between family traditions and healthy flexibility. In the second chapter, I indicated four firmly held traditions of our early generations: Irish-American, Catholic, Democratic, and Northern. More flexibility became evident in recent generations. To me, one general conclusion became transparent as Irish crystal: we've come a long way from County Kerry. As storyteller, I'll now look at the more flexible family traditions from my viewpoint. However, some relatives may not share all of my views.

The Irish-American tradition. I'm an American with Irish background, and thanks to positive melting pot experiences, I also respect and support the ethnic and racial traditions of others. My attraction to Irish culture embraces literature, song, travel, the original *Riverdance*, and now Ireland via the Internet. I made a list of Irish films scattered in many areas of my favorite video store. Responding to my suggestion, the manager made a special section containing thirty-four Irish films on the shelves already featuring Australian, English, French, German, and other foreign categories. While browsing in the video store on St. Patrick's Day, I heard the manager on the phone with a customer: "Yes, we have a section for Irish films, not just today but all year long, come in and look around there." I instinctively gestured with a Roger Ebert thumbs-up to the manager when he hung up the phone, and he returned the gesture.

For years I've enjoyed short stories and other works of Irish writers Frank O'Connor and Sean O'Faolain and tried in vain to buy my own copy of *The Collected Stories of Sean O'Faolain* by searching in used bookstores. In the meantime, I took this 1,300-page book out of the same library every year. I finally sent a desperate letter to the librarian and offered to pay $50.00 for the old book. She sent a long letter about the philosophy of a library in service to the common good. The bottom line was no sale so I decided to make my plea in person.

"We can't possibly put this on the shelf of books-for-sale," she said, after a check of computer records. "You can see on the computer that it has gone out once each year for many years."

"Oh, that would be charges made to my library card," I said, knowing that a Catch-22 was now developing. "You mean if I hadn't taken out the book, then I could buy it now?"

"That's right, but we don't keep the names, only the number count. We can't be sure that you alone used the book."

I gave up, but noticed that a distant library had a copy. The next day I called the librarian in a rural area of the county. "I know you're generally short on funds so I'm willing to pay $75.00 for *The Collected Stories of Sean O'Faolain*, because...," I started my plea. Interrupting my rehearsed offer, she shouted through the phone, "Sold!" This book now stands in attention next to a similar collection of stories by Frank O'Connor on the shelf of my bookcase reserved for Irish literature, Irish history, and travel in Ireland.

Most of the time, I'm an American with faint Irish background. Readers may find this hard to believe, but I go for months and seasons without reference to Ireland and things Irish. Yet, some primordial part of me resonates with Irish culture. When I see, or hear, or experience genuine Irish culture, in any art form, I come alive. I find the difference between Irish culture and Irish kitsch by my educated toe test. In the film *Dancing at Lughnasa*, there was a delightful scene where four sisters danced in the yard while the prim and controlled oldest sister, played by Meryl Streep, watched with disapproval. Then the camera cut to her toe, which ever so slightly began to move and then to tap. Soon she irresistibly joined in the dance. When my educated toe begins to tap, I recognize genuine Irish culture in any art form. I sense that I'm no longer in America, but magically and inexplicably at *home* and irresistibly dancing at Lughnasa.

Others have experienced this feeling of being at *home* in Ireland. Irish-American author Sally Quinn, stated in the quarterly *The World of Hibernia*: "It's something that I sense very deeply. It flows out of the intense feeling that, in Ireland, I am home." Her insight helped to explain the healthy state of Irish tourism and the mystery of thousands of Irish-Americans of different generations returning *home* again to cities and villages all over Ireland, even though most were born in America perhaps generations after their ancestors immigrated to the U.S.

My moderate mind kept reminding me that I had celebrated the positives of Irish and Irish-Americans and pressed me to confess candidly the counterbalancing negatives. I did this gingerly, not as a know-it-all. Sometimes I sensed that Irish-American tourists had less interest in serious Celtic art and more concern with sentimental souvenirs.

Some Irish-Americans have flaunted their ethnicity and been insensitive to other ethnic and racial traditions. Early Irish immigrants to America endured insults, discrimination, and oppression, but some of their descendants, by a collective amnesia, have been uncaring to new ethnic or racial groups. In a similar way, some Irish-Americans have reflected little sensitivity toward those of different religious beliefs.

And still others have equated Irish genius and culture with the pouring of Guinness beer, despite the graphic witness of Frank McCourt to suffering in some Irish families, stemming from alcohol abuse and alcoholism. Some have refined grudge keeping to the point of this joke: What is Irish Alzheimer's? The Irish forget everything but their grudges. But that's enough about the negatives.

Coming from Irish background rarely made a difference for me in my work. But I'll never forget a face-to-face meeting with a government bureaucrat in his small cubicle.

"Are the Cuddys from Tipperary Hill in Syracuse?" he conspiratorially whispered.

"Well, I'm from the Cuddys and Hartigans of County Kerry, and my family settled first in Pennsylvania and then in Endicott, but that was a long time ago," I said.

He looked at me for almost twenty seconds, and I imagined that he might be thinking, "Did he say County Kerry? If so, that is good enough for me."

"Did you say County Kerry?"

"Yes, I come from mountainy people, so I've been told, and I've hiked in County Kerry to the top of MacGillycuddy's Reeks, the highest point in Ireland."

"Well, that's good enough for me. I'm from Tipperary Hill." This chat was more effective than a secret Masonic handshake in some other wildly opposite context. Placing a form into his typewriter, he said, "Glad to help one of our lads. Instead of putting this on the slow track, I can start your form right now." I felt for a moment that I was somewhere else. It seemed that I was in Mayor Curley's Boston City Hall.

Although I wasn't from Tipperary Hill in Syracuse, I knew some of its legends. Tipp Hill's long history covered the wide spectrum from stone-throwing teens to dramatic readings from James Joyce. The traffic light there has featured green on top and red on bottom for decades. This goes back to the insistence of the Tipperary Hill youths on that arrangement. Whenever Syracuse City Hall installed a conventional light, the toughs with the unambiguous name – they had no identity crisis – of "The Stone Throwers" broke the signal. City Hall finally gave in, and the practice of green-over-red continues to this day. A street sculpture for several years has featured a bronze father pointing to the actual traffic light to teach his bronze children the tradition of "The Stone Throwers." A few years ago, the remaining Stone Throwers, by then senior citizens and folk heroes, led the St. Patrick's Day parade in Syracuse.

Pete Coleman, publican and landlord of Coleman's Pub, has provided a place on Tipperary Hill for Irish music and song. Members of the Syracuse James Joyce Society have read hours of the complex and challenging *Ulysses* every Bloomsday, June 16, at Coleman's or other pubs on the Hill. Joyce and I've visited Tipp Hill for the readings on annual Bloomsday. The Irish Diaspora has been of special interest to me. Tipp Hill was one example of scattered Irish-American women and men engaging in song and revelry, and listening to the magical words of Irish writers. There are Irish focal points in many cities around the world, each with its own shade of green.

I never claimed to speak for the complex Irish people, those in Ireland or elsewhere, such as Irish-Americans or Americans with Irish background. Because the millennium was a time for new beginnings and many religious, racial, and cultural apologies, I fashioned a small prayer for this book: "Oh God, forgive my Irish excesses. Forgive the Irish excesses of my family of seven generations." All other Irish and Irish-Americans, people by turns witty, gabby, articulate, garrulous, eloquent, and chattering, can and will speak for themselves.

Catholic But More Flexible

The Catholic tradition. Against the historical background of church changes, I have understood more fully my own religious development. In the early generations of my immigrant clan, family members adhered more rigidly to their Catholic traditions and regulations. However, as the immigrant church grew and developed, my family became more adaptive and flexible, especially after the reforms and renewal of the Vatican Council II, 1962-1965.

In sharing how I'm a Catholic Christian today, I've tried to strike a balance between an overly detached account and a too personal one. Joyce, other advisers, and I discussed ways to keep my views within the framework and tonality of family storytelling where possible. I carefully share my opinions on some current hot-button church issues, but without banging on the bully pulpit of this book. I offer the viewpoint of a family storyteller, married priest, and sixty-seven year-old *elder* in the Catholic Church.

I'm grateful for the many sacraments and blessings that I've received from the Catholic Church during my lifetime. I'm happy to have been ordained a priest and also to have married Joyce. In return, I've sought to be a Catholic Christian with commitment to public worship with the community, now at a moderate-to-liberal parish. I believe in Jesus, the center of my faith, and His essential gospel teachings about loving God and loving neighbor. Moreover, as a Catholic of the post-immigrant church, I appreciate the reforms and renewal of the Vatican Council II, and I encourage fuller implementation of these reforms, found in the sixteen decrees of the Council with real, not rubber-stamp, representation of lay women and men in an open process. The fuller implementation of Council renewal and reforms is an ongoing process.

There are many models of church, and I'm grateful for the church as home for sinners. The church as home borrows the idea from Robert Frost that: "Home is the place where, when you have to go there, they have to take you in." I place my bet on the mercy of God and value my membership in the church because it is the inclusive home of sinners, not a fortress for excluding others. The church is at its best when it finds gospel, flexible, and pastoral reasons to include, rather than exclude, people in its membership and at its altar table. I also admire and support the servant model of church that reaches out to the poor, marginalized, and isolated.

Joyce and I belong to the liberal Call to Action movement and admire the centrist Voice of the Faithful, founded recently in Boston. Both groups, in different ways, urge a Vatican Council II type of church. The *National Catholic Reporter*, an independent and progressive newspaper, has come weekly in the mail for decades, and I value most of its articles. I look first for the column of lighthearted and wise columnist, Tim Unsworth. His skillful mix of humor, wisdom, and religion encouraged me to blend lighthearted and serious tones in my style of storytelling.

"Did you read Tim Unsworth's current column?" I've often asked Joyce.

"Yes, it reminded me of you. You're a worthy Unsworthian Catholic," she said several times, knowing how I agree with his merciful, pastoral positions salted with humor and wit.

As our family has evolved, so have our Catholic traditions. While my ancestors were probably more on the conservative end, I'm a liberal Catholic, but not an extreme one. I wish that all fellow Catholics would openly define themselves on the Catholic spectrum: liberal, centrist, conservative. There are strengths and weaknesses in each of these positions. Catholics from these three camps sooner or later must learn to dialogue with one another toward a tolerant, common ground model of church. Cardinal Joseph Bernardin of Chicago urged common ground dialogue before he died. Interaction with civility and charity is lacking today among many Catholics. I'm not trying to force conservatives and centrists into accepting my liberal positions. My concern is to clarify my liberal approaches and to remain open to other Catholics of different angles of vision.

I noted above that over twenty-five years ago after a discernment process, I made serious decisions to resign from the priesthood and marry Joyce. The theology of Israel in the Babylonian exile has given spiritual meaning to me and 20,000 other American married priests now in exile. This amazing statistic comes from a 2002 *Meet the Press* TV program, and others put the number even higher. The worldwide figure is more than 100,000 exiled married priests. Should the church not look for alternative ways to resolve the serious clergy shortage and the closing or combining of parishes nationwide? Some priests are circuit riders to multiple parishes led by dedicated lay leaders or sisters, but this is a weak and temporary solution.

I admit my bias in favor of optional celibacy and the freedom to marry. Mandatory celibacy for Catholic clergy is a church discipline, not a doctrine, and is changeable. A thoughtful discussion, including all levels of the church, about optional celibacy is past due. Marriage is not a cure-all for life or for the priesthood and would bring its own challenges for married priests. However, the benefits would far outweigh any negatives in my opinion. Both celibate priests and married priests with differing gifts can serve the People of God.

I'm not a single voice calling for public debate on optional celibacy. The organization of married American priests, Corpus, has been advocating this reform for over thirty years. By the spring of 2004, some priests in several American dioceses have publicly petitioned for discussion of optional celibacy. In fairness, I report that some priests of one diocese developed a joint letter supporting mandatory celibacy. A few American bishops also have recently expressed their support for discussion on optional celibacy. There is also a recent precedent for married priests that merits our focus: the Catholic Church welcomes converting Episcopalian priests with their wives into Catholic priestly ministry in America and elsewhere.

A brief look at the sex abuse by clergy scandal seemed unavoidable because of the general awareness and concern of most Americans, Catholic or other. That some priests abused minors and that some bishops placed sex-abusing priests and the reputation of the church before the welfare of children, teens, and some adults has outraged and discouraged many. The healing of sex abuse victims and their families must be the top priority for bishops, priests, sisters, and laity. The church is striving to assure parents of the present and future security of minors through formal safety programs. A church culture of transparency and accountability is being required by an angry laity. This new culture reflects the gospels of Jesus more than the discredited approach of excessive secrecy. The church as home of sinners can help us to understand the complex crisis of sex abuse and other related and unrelated urgent issues.

For decades, American bishops have had a strong track record of supporting social justice, immigrants, Catholic Charities programs, and Catholic Relief Services for the poor overseas. However, the National Review Board (comprised of lay women and men) reported on the sex abuse crisis in 2004 and severely criticized bishops for a number of reasons. The outspoken National Review Board Report as well as the John Jay Report on statistics of sex abuse by priests can be found on the Website – Conference of Catholic Bishops: www.usccb.org. Another resource for reviewing the ongoing crisis from newspapers and journals in America and around the world can be found at the *National Catholic Reporter* Website: www.ncronline.org. Click on the Abuse Tracker box. Every day some articles report news, and others are reflective and analytical.

Clericalism was criticized in the National Review Board Report: "Finally the haughty attitude of some bishops, which has exacerbated the crisis, is a byproduct of clericalism. Just as priests are often placed on a pedestal far above the laity they serve, certain bishops appear far removed from their priests" (104-106). From the seminary onward we were exposed to the virulent virus of clericalism with its unhealthy features of special treatment, privilege, and high pedestals for the clergy. Many priests and some bishops, to their credit, have been discerning enough, and gospel-oriented enough, to struggle throughout their lives against the virus of clericalism and have kept it in remission.

I share a personal observation. Nothing has been so effectively curative of clericalism and "pedestalization" in my life as my marriage to Joyce. We belong to a network of more than sixty married priests and their wives living in the Syracuse diocese. I've noticed, sometimes out of the corner of my eye, and admired how these wives assisted in eradicating any residual pedestalization in their husbands. I'm sure they, in turn, saw how Joyce encouraged my growth away from lingering clericalism. Some day the church may be humble enough to dialogue with priests' wives, such as Joyce, Meme, Maureen, Pat, Gloria, Heather, Fran, etc., and be open to their experience and wisdom.

Joyce and I have concern for the vast majority of blameless priests. Some are our abiding friends of more than forty years, and we support and encourage them. Moreover, accused priests have a right to due process in civil law and in church law. Joyce and I share the pain that victims with their families, dedicated priests and sisters, and laity feel. The church, as people of God, will be working for years to achieve complex healing for victims directly and for all Catholics indirectly. The fundamental belief of Christians is in the death and resurrection of Jesus. I believe that the priesthood and the church, after a long struggling time, will rise again in new, renewed, and I believe, surprising ways.

From Joyce, spouses of inactive priests, other laywomen, and religious sisters, I've learned more fully about the opinions, accomplishments, and disappointments of some women in the church. These mostly centrist and liberal women were well educated and articulate about opposing sexism in church and society. Patriarchal attitudes and actions of church leaders have caused them suffering. Sexism in church and society is found in America, Ireland, and everywhere else.

I carefully picked the chapter quote from the "Madeleva Manifesto" and the following quotation from Sister Joan Chittister from her book *In Search of Belief.* She sees some ways out of sexism: "The fact is that nothing will really change in the way the world goes together until we change the language, until we learn to think differently, until we learn to see women as an equal image of God and the image of God as birthing mother, loving spirit, passionate compassion, heart of justice, and womb of the universe." Against the background of her fresh thinking and that of others, is it such a stretch to support gender equality in the church and specifically an inclusive Catholic priesthood of women and men, married and celibate? Without some new approaches, some Catholics will suffer from the shortage of male and celibate priests. They will become spiritually emaciated with an unsatisfied hunger for the Eucharistic food and drink of Jesus.

In writing this book, I discovered that my support for women in church and society stemmed partially from a family predisposition. Our family stories supply a list of strong and independent women. There are examples from each generation: Famine survivor Hartigan; benign matriarch Margaret Dean; Grandma Harriet Cawley, probable conspirator involved in disrupting the Ku Klux Klan parade; Mom Veronica Cuddy, assertive wife and mother; wife Joyce Cuddy, dedicated school teacher; niece Becky Parham, strong teacher and a leader of a refugee settlement project; and grandniece Caroline Parham, already an active member of youth programs at church.

I can't ask opinions of the above deceased ancestors from the first to fourth generations, but I've guessed that as strong women they would've supported, if given the opportunity, women's equality in church and society. I know that Joyce and Becky support equality and justice for women; I've heard them discussing these issues. Caroline already has her opinions on women's rights; I know because I asked her recently.

A final suggestion has been perking in my mind for a long time. I again join others when I encourage a paradigm change in tonality whereby the church focuses less on sexual morality, bound in prohibitions. Many people practically define Catholics in terms of strict negative sexual ethics and miss the rich and wide context of the good news of Jesus and the Catholic faith. Would not a more balanced church result if Catholics were defined, by themselves and others, for their love of God and neighbor and other gospel teachings of Jesus?

Sexuality is complex and can be abused and exploited in ways damaging to adults, teens, and children. I'm not a Pollyanna about this complex issue. Even so, sexual morality with fewer negatives and more positives can be taught with an emphasis on balanced, healthy, and positive methods. Married Catholics with conscientious experience and long-ignored wisdom in sexuality can enrich sexual ethics and teaching methods.

"Amen," I say, leaving the bully pulpit with hope and prayer for the now and future church, but also with realism about its serious and ongoing challenges. My hope for a renewed and reformed church is not flabby wishful thinking. I look to Studs Terkel, in *Hope Dies Last*, for the right kind of hope: "Hope is born of activism, commitment, and the steely determination to resist."

Democrats Still, But Not All

The Democratic tradition. Since age twenty-one, I've voted for Democrats most of the time. I strongly concur with liberal and social justice principles of the Democratic Party. At age fifty, I voted for a Republican coworker for county legislator. I felt anxiety when I pulled the lever in the voting booth. "So this is how one feels betraying family and the Democratic Party," I said to myself. I made a special point to tell the victorious Republican, at our next meeting, about my vote and family tradition. We laughed, but my ancestors in Calvary Cemetery near Endicott were not laughing. When Dave disclosed some votes for Republicans, Mom, who worked at the polling table on Election Day, muttered to me, but she didn't challenge him. Full democracy begrudgingly came to our family in the fifth generation.

Northern Tradition ~ Four Seasons Preference

The Northern tradition. I'm a Northerner for most of the year. Joyce and I go south during winter to a rental unit in Florida. We enjoy ethnic restaurants, especially Wolfie Cohen's Jewish restaurant, and the large Hispanic culture in south Florida. After shopping for the right ideological Catholic parish, we found one in Pompano Beach named for San Isidro with lively singing, leisurely Sunday liturgy (ninety minutes), and unabashed friendliness. The parish has a good mix of Hispanics, African-Americans, and Anglos and many comprehensive service programs for the needy.

Kitsch and culture are mixed in unusual ways in south Florida. There are many museums, art galleries, and theaters. On the other hand, a famous flea market by day has thirteen drive-in screens in its huge parking lot for first-run movies by night.

"There's our Stonehenge," I've said to Joyce whenever we passed the dramatic configuration of tall outdoor screens. Centuries from now, archeologists might argue that the excavated ruins of one of the thirteen movie screens lines up with the sun at dawn on summer solstice day.

We retired in 1995, and retirement years are gifts and opportunities for grace. Health has been a key factor in retirement, and we are grateful for the benefit of Medicare. Joyce and I are more conscious of death and we recognize more names in the obituaries. We have volunteered up north in helping agencies, Joyce in a hospital, and I in a senior center and library. We volunteered down south as well. I've helped in a library in a poor neighborhood, and Joyce tutored a lively first grader in English. Patrick spoke Polish, German, and some English and made remarkable progress in reading and speaking English with coaching from Joyce. Our Polish friends, John, Bozena, Patricia, Michael, Janina, Patrick, Lars, Joanna, Jeff, and Bartlomiej have enriched us with their Polish foods and culture. We remember with Christian prayer young Krzysztof Kaminski who died recently.

Joyce and I've driven back north in early March. In transit we visited the sixth and seventh generations in North Carolina, and the youth of Caroline and Carter has renewed us. We usually found the first snow on the ground in Maryland, more snow in the Pocono Mountains of Pennsylvania, and enough snow back home for us to downhill ski a few days. The warming March sun has followed us north. Maple sap began to run, crocuses poked through the lingering snow, and Joyce's daffodils flashed their gold and defied the frost. I fished within a week of ice out on the lakes, and honking Canada geese flew north in huge "V's" written across the blue denim sky of spring. We've been glad to return home in East Syracuse, because Joyce and I, like some of our family members, remain Northerners. Mysteries of the four seasons course in our blood.

Daydreaming About Caroline and Carter's Future

Most seniors, I presume, daydream about the future of their families. Just as I had to imagine details for some early generations, I projected in a playful way the future of our family. What is important is that family members have the opportunity to follow their stars. I trust that Caroline and Carter of the seventh generation will foster openness and growth in the eighth generation in future years. The American family of ethnic inclusions will likely increase free and multiethnic generations, which, by the melting pot mix, will overcome ancient human separations and hatreds. The positive elements of Irish pride will hopefully remain one influence in the complex mix of our ongoing family.

In my daydream, Caroline's youngest daughter Cara, in late high school, said to her, "I've decided on Duke U. for pre-med and med school with a specialty in Organ Transplants. But I know you dislike Duke."

"Our family members have been dedicated alumni of North Carolina University, arch rival of Duke, for more than seventy years," Caroline explained. "It would be hard for us to even imagine you at Duke. You could go somewhere else."

"But Duke specializes in organ transplants and the mix-and-match, cut-and-paste medicine that I want to pursue," Cara said. "Think of all the older folks who participated in the recent AARP Organ-Donors' 10K Walk. I want to help similar aged people in need of transplants."

"Okay, okay," Caroline said. "Let me talk to your father. Our family has changed before."

On another occasion I daydreamed in detail of Carter. He married a Spanish artist, and they settled in Japan. They've easily visited their relatives in Greensboro, North Carolina and Barcelona on newer and faster jet planes; some carry over a thousand passengers.

"We fly east to west when going around the world from Japan to Mombai in India to Barcelona to New York to Greensboro to Seattle to Japan again. But we fly west to east when going around the world from Japan to Seattle to Greensboro to New York to Barcelona to Mombai to Japan again," said Carter. "It's a question of whose family we visit first."

Carter's son Carlos, I daydreamed, won a soccer scholarship and studied languages at Tokyo University. He took courses in Spanish and Italian to honor some of his roots. During the summer after his junior year, he visited Ireland for a smattering of the Gaelic language and culture. He also climbed to the top of MacGillycuddy's Reeks to validate another part of his complex roots.

Winding Down

These were my daydreams, but others would have different dreams about our family's future. Only time will tell how our family of seven generations will grow and develop. Future generations may continue with family traditions or they may break from them. Our family has changed before and will keep changing. But I hope that some future family members will be able to make the trip to Ireland and visit MacGillycuddy's Reeks in County Kerry to touch their Irish roots. My final wishes are that family members never forget where they came from and that our tradition of family storytelling continues, with new storytellers to keep it going. Their Irish heritage will remain as one of many strong, prideful roots.

After reviewing the seven chapters on seven generations and imagining briefly the eighth, I'm confident that I'll continue to watch, listen, remember, and write family tales. I'm open to late-breaking family stories, but feel no pressure to neatly tie up all generational loose ends.

I watched a TV interview about Jean Butler, the leaping female lead in the original troop of *Riverdance*. I had seen her flights of dancing and was struck by her airy performances. She somehow defied gravity. In the interview Ms. Butler told of being asked by a friend how she would prefer to die. "In the air!" she said, without hesitation. I loved her creative and wise response. I would answer the same question: "While telling or writing family stories."

Joyce and I, winding down in our senior years, now hold our concern for family yarns and for life itself with a loose grip. We accept the slowing down of the rhythms of our lives, but we try to keep active. After recently viewing televised relay races at a track meet, we combined efforts on this metaphor: We have handed on the baton in the race of life, and the future is in the hands of our younger relatives with their firmer grasp and swifter pace. Trusting them as they run toward the future in a world where freedom is strong and the inclusive teachings of Jesus are increasingly expanding, Joyce and I are peaceful, confident, and free.

"The family tradition of fishing has been passed on."
Left to right: Carter, Jim, and Caroline, 1999.

"Dave died on his own terms, in bed, at home.
He was his own man in life and death."
Picture in 1985 and death in 1997.

Epilogue

A Theater Fantasy:
Spirit of MacGillycuddy's Reeks

"When you are old and gray and full of sleep,
And nodding by the fire, take down this book,
And slowly read, and dream of the soft look
Your eyes had once, and of their shadows deep;"

William Butler Yeats, "When You Are Old"

Epilogue: Theater Fantasy

Curtain rises on the stage with a panoramic backdrop of MacGillycuddy's Reeks in County Kerry and no other props. I wish that I had the power to summon everybody, including the large Irish chorus of singing family spirits to the stage for a final bow. Instead, I chose to imagine representatives from the seven generations coming to the stage. Each generation embodied a different ideal and added something to our family. Our ancestors live on in us, and hopefully we will live on in our future descendents and pass on our wisdom to them.

The start of our family as we know it – my Great-great-grandmother Hartigan of the first generation, a Famine survivor – enters the stage. Wearing a traditional dark dress with a bow and veil, she brings with her courage. She came to a new world with nothing and persevered, which launched our family history.

Boisterous Great-grandfather Thomas McDermott of the second generation enters exuding confidence. He wears spats, an Aran knit cardigan, a skimmer straw hat, and he carries a black hawthorn walking stick. He embodies pride – for his surroundings, his family, and most of all for his heritage.

Extraordinary grandfather, Joe Cawley of the third generation, enters in his plumbing uniform of blue denim bib-overalls and work shirt. He carries a brown papier-mâché rocking chair and playfully throws it into the audience. Joe carries with him the ideals of hard work. He appreciated manual labor and wasn't afraid to get his hands dirty.

Parents John and Veronica Cuddy of the fourth generation enter and dance a turn around the stage to the tune of their song "Margie." They embody the notion of gratitude. They were no strangers to hardship. Though they hardly had anything during the time of the Depression, they knew that others had less, and they were thankful for what they did have.

Brother Dave Cuddy of the fifth generation enters wearing a business suit, the traditional white shirt, and conservative tie of IBM employees. Dave brings with him determination. He pursued his dreams of rising to higher levels at IBM, even though it meant a break from family traditions, namely our Northern tradition. His persistence and dedication allowed him to rise to the top.

Nieces Becky and Carolyn from the sixth generation enter the stage wearing colorful bell-bottoms and tie-dyed tops of the 1970s. They embody strength. Though Carolyn was lost to us at a young age, her death brought out the strength of our family. Becky took the dream of being a teacher that they both had shared and made it a reality.

Grandniece Caroline gracefully dances onto the stage, and grandnephew Carter, with his baseball hat and bat, follows. They are the members of the seventh generation. They bring with them hope – hope for our family's future. We trust them to keep our family alive and to pass on their Irish, Italian, and Scots-Irish traditions.

Finally, I enter holding the hand of my wife and soul mate Joyce. We are both from the fifth generation. I enter with joy – joy in my family and traditions, joy that I was able to bring the members together, and joy that our future generations, by reading this book, will be able to glimpse into their past.

All form a semicircle around Great-great-grandmother Hartigan. She presents copies of this book of family stories to Caroline and Carter. "We know that you have other branches of your family, but you'll learn some of our stories and ways in this book," she says to them in a strong voice. "Our hopes for the future are in your hands, and we trust you to find your own ways."

I appreciate the wisdom of this first generation elder about non-possessive love, and my memory serves up a favorite quote from *In the Spirit, In the Flesh*, by Eugene Kennedy. I share it with the family: "The person…that believes in non-possessive love must also believe in letting people have lives of their own. This is as hard a thing as there is in life: the willing realization that our children, our loved ones, or our friends are not our possessions." All nod in agreement.

"Thank you for our books, my…," Caroline pauses and mentally traces her relationship to Grandmother Hartigan, "Great-great-great-great grandmother Hartigan."

Thomas McDermott is happy to get into the act. "An Irish stew pot to remember the Famine, a pot-of-gold to recall our family's economic struggle and growth, and a melting pot to depict our family's ethnic development," he says, dramatically reading the engraved words on a plaque with three small bronze vessels decorated with swirly Celtic art. He gives one plaque to Caroline and another to Carter.

Caroline helps Carter recall his long name, spanning from the seventh to the second generations. Carter nods and says confidently, "Thanks, Great-great-great-grandfather McDermott, for our plaques."

Caroline and Carter kiss all of the assembled relatives. Their ancestors wave supportively and wistfully as they run offstage and toward the future. "Run, Caroline! Run, Carter!" I whisper to Joyce.

The stage lights flicker amid the sounds of uilleann pipes and bodrahn drums, and singing and laughter offstage. Older relatives understand at once the source of merriment.

"Are those the benign and merry family spirits that I heard on top of The Reeks in Ireland?" I ask, seeking to verify my hunch.

"Of course they are, Seamus," Joe Cawley replies. All listen until the spirits gradually fall silent and the lights begin to dim.

"It's been a long way from County Kerry to upstate New York for the northern branch and to North Carolina for the southern branch," Dave says.

"It's been a demanding, adventuresome, and at times, lighthearted journey. The adventure continues," adds Becky, the family storyteller in waiting.

All the principals join hands to make a final bow. Our family bow is unlike the bow of the precision dancers, The Rockettes in New York's Radio City Music Hall. In testimony to the glorious imperfections of our unrehearsed and uneven family life, some bow with full-bows, others with half-bows, and others with simple quarter-bows. The relatives leave the stage, and the panoramic backdrop of MacGillycuddy's Reeks is the last thing seen as the curtain and lights fall simultaneously. And so the sharing of family stories of seven generations ends where it began, with those enchanted Reeks, visited now and again by family spirits and bathed in soft and magical light.

Jim's pack, stick and hat in foreground; top of
MacGillycuddy's Reeks, left of hat, in background, 1999.

Not So Much The End, As So Far

"'It's been a demanding, adventuresome, and at times, lighthearted journey. The adventure continues,' adds Becky, the family storyteller in waiting." 2003.

"…as they run offstage and toward the future. 'Run, Caroline! Run, Carter!' I whisper to Joyce." 2000.

Appendix

And How to Write Your Family Tales

"You must learn — and for some reason you often have to relearn — how to churn out words whether or not you feel in tune with what you're writing. The precondition for writing well is being able to write badly and to write when you are not in the mood."

Peter Elbow, Writing With Power

I informally wove suggestions about writing family stories into the first chapter. Now I share ten formal hints. There are many approaches to family storytelling and story writing, each with different strengths and weaknesses. These suggestions worked for me and demonstrate one way, but not the only way, to gather, organize, and write family stories. I wanted to avoid a too tutorial approach in giving advice. Readers can zig and zag with my hints and find their own way.

♣ *Hint One* ♣

Read in the fields of family history, storytelling, memoir, autobiography, and biography. Then decide what form to use. I began writing a dry family history, but found the form wasn't right and switched to family storytelling. In addition, finding my voice, modeled on my Cawley grandparents, was a process of discovery. After that the most basic, yet most difficult challenge was to tell universal stories of interest to a wide audience. Please, try not to brag about the family.

♣ *Hint Two* ♣

Find the existing family research. I valued Dad's carefully developed family tree from the second to sixth generations, even though it didn't have dates and only had the names of our ancestors by generation. Aunt Jule's family records from her Bible were a godsend. At my request, niece Becky gave me copies of some records that I couldn't easily find in my loose files. My own records eventually surfaced, and I learned, in part, the timesaving value of organized files. Joyce groans at my idiosyncratic system of piles of paper files. However, my computer files are better.

My recent symbolic trip to Ireland was energizing and mind-expanding. Motivated by Irish travel and especially the enchanted-religious-literary experience of singing spirits on The Reeks, I began to outline chapters, one for each generation. Even so, it's not necessary for family storytellers and writers to make a costly trip to their ancestral land. Books, travel videos, magazines, and Internet data can help those unable to travel abroad for general background or specific family research. The point is to know as much about your geographical root culture as possible.

♣ *Hint Three* ♣

Use attractive photos, bright photos, and few photos. Less is more. Every family has one or two lifelong photographers with many albums and boxes of loose pictures. Aunt Jule, family photographer as well as designated storyteller, gave to Dave and me custom-made generational albums for our fiftieth birthdays. Mom also saved boxes of pictures. Some photos were small, wrinkled, and damaged, but these flaws enhanced the sense of history.

Because some publishers prefer black and white photos, I converted colored pictures of recent generations to black and white. This gave a consistent feel to the past and the present. Of course, colored pictures could be used to complement older black and whites. Placing few pictures on a given photo-page insures lots of surrounding white space and reduces distracting clutter.

In brief, be selective about the quality and quantity of photos. Some pictures might be too sentimental for wider viewing. After sifting through hundreds of pictures, I ran my selection of photos and exhibits by Joyce and others for their evaluation and opinion.

♣ *Hint Four* ♣

Choose literary quotes carefully to set the tone for each chapter and additional quotes to enhance the text; I tried to strike a balance between too many and too few quotations. I was also committed to using relevant quotes from a variety of sources, though not every favorite quotation can fit into generational storytelling. Although I chose a literary approach to some topics, others might choose different formats.

My three visits to Ireland and especially the hike up MacGillycuddy's Reeks deeply influenced me, consciously and probably unconsciously, to use extensive Irish tonality. Others might choose less ethnic tones. First-generation immigrants clustered together for mutual support and for maintaining the old country's language and customs. Later generations at first ignored their roots and then gradually rekindled an interest in visiting the country of family origin and ethnic traditions. That general theory has helped me in the fifth generation to understand my interest in Irish and Irish-American culture.

♣ *Hint Five* ♣

The hard work of transforming a rough outline into well-rounded stories takes time. Don't delay writing until the end of the research period. Drafting stories stimulated my memory to bubble up many additional yarns, related and unrelated, but I soon learned that not every meaningful and positive memory was worth including. Use the "Delete" key on the computer often in the process of writing, rewriting, and editing.

Find the best time for creative writing. In retirement I had more options for extended writing times. I discovered that, as a night person, I enjoyed creative writing more from nine to midnight than from nine to noon. So I wrote my creative pages at night and did the equally important grunt work of editing and rewriting in the morning. The discipline of sitting before the computer and concentrating kept my brain cells firing in retirement.

Don't throw away your dictionaries because your computer has spell-check. Andy Rooney is famous for consulting multiple dictionaries and works on grammar and style. Though I used computer spell-check, I also used two current dictionaries for words not covered by my computer.

In generational writing, I found that keeping the time frames clean was not possible. Relatives don't live and die within a neat chapter for each generation. Most characters overlap other generations.

♣ *Hint Six* ♣

Use a computer or word processor to make revisions and corrections easier. James Joyce left many handwritten manuscripts with cross-outs and corrections in the margins, which have bedeviled scholars. A computer with electronic files would have made his writing much easier and scholars much happier. Computer writing also allows for many rewrites. A computer would have helped Frank O'Connor, Irish short story writer. His lifelong revising of short stories on his typewriter was legendary and would have been less laborious if he had lived in the age of computers. Young writers are familiar with computers and word processing from an early age, but some senior writers might be tentative about learning to use computers for writing family stories. I strongly recommend them.

On the downside, seemingly endless revisions by a writer can wring all the creative juices out of the writing. After many rewrites and much editing, I finally said, "Yes, yes, yeeees! I'm done. I'll spoil it by making any more revisions." When I pushed the "Print" key for the last time, I felt satisfied, and Joyce and I shared a champagne toast.

♣ *Hint Seven* ♣

Get feedback on chapter drafts from thoughtful and frank friends. This keeps the writer grounded in reality. Critical readers are necessary for corrections as well as for suggestions, especially in the blind spots of the writer. I owe thanks to Robert Emmet Long, author and editor of more than forty books and a James Joyce scholar; he sent a letter of encouragement when I was losing confidence. My thoughts went from how did I ever get into this project to how in the world do I get out of it, but changing moods are part of a writer's world.

Be open to critics without defensiveness. I was so close to the writing that, at times, I needed evaluations from others to gain perspective. Occasional breaks from the work in progress can be creative. I took breaks of six weeks, two months, three months, and four months. After breaks I came back to the text with fresh eyes and new creativity.

The family story writer needs to balance personal viewpoints with those of others, especially in stories about his/her own generation. I was challenged in the fifth generation chapter to counterbalance my stories with tales about Dave, Carlo, Dusty, Sister Mary Frances, Rose Marie, Fran, Donna, Clara, Orangie, Ray, and others with their different points of view. How well I accomplished this difficult challenge for balance, I leave for the readers to judge. I tried also to respect Dad's embellishing, Mom's sanitizing, Dave's darkening, and my tendency to lighten our family tales. Perhaps a few stories were influenced by all four until they reached their final written form

♣ *Hint Eight* ♣

Most of those trying to use the family storytelling form may end with a private book or booklet for family use, and family members, present and future, will be grateful. For those who pursue possible publication, I suggest the writer evaluate the many possibilities, including cyber-publication, now available. I finally opted for the route of query letter to publisher, then outline with sample chapters when requested, then full book with photos when directed. It was a journey of a few years for me from the first written word to a published work. I'm planning another book about the wit and wisdom of wives of priests (over 20,000 in the U.S.).

It helps to have a track record of published works, but every writer starts as an unpublished novice. I have more than a dozen published articles to my credit and two published short stories in the fiction category, since 1979. Some were in national markets, the *National Catholic Reporter* and *National Fisherman*; others in regional markets, *Avenue M* in Chicago, *Chapel Hill Newspaper* in North Carolina, *Catskill Mountain News* in New York; and some in local markets, *The Post Standard* in Syracuse, and *Talk of the Towns* in Endicott. My topics included hiking, fishing, humor, religion, and social justice themes. A list of writing credits can be attached to query letters to publishers; this helps you to get a foot in the door.

♣ *Hint Nine* ♣

Have patience with the publishing process. Upon completion of this book, I put my energies into writing query letters to publishers and avoided mailbox watching. Any pestering of editor and publisher is counterproductive. Letters of rejection did not discourage me; I revised my queries and tried new strategies. A suggestion: rejection letters make good starters for the fireplace on cold nights. The huge annual *Writer's Market* (1,112 pages in 2001) has an honest price for the weight; this fat book shares data on hundreds of publishers, agents, and their needs, as well as dozens of helpful tips from successful writers of different ages.

♣ *Hint Ten And Final Advice* ♣

Writing generational family stories became for me a form of spiritual journal writing. The total context of my life and family history became clear. A family story writer processes the past, distills wisdom, shares the results, and is open to the future. I also found that the process was a healthy way to prepare for death. As a senior citizen, I now read the obituaries with more than casual interest.

I'm confident that the journal writing aspect of generational storytelling gives a healthy balance to one's life that is often unavailable for many during their last months and final stay in the hospital with all the new medications, long wires, curved tubes, electronic bells, and digital whistles. This healthy balance can reduce unproductive anxieties and needless fears that often harry the minds of even good people toward the end of their lives. I'm convinced that a book or booklet of family stories and a family album would help those receiving final care in hospitals or in praiseworthy and practical Hospice programs.

At the risk of appearing morbid, I've asked Joyce to place this book in my casket. Not soon I trust. In this way, I'll hit the ground running in the world of the hereafter and have with me a resource, like a program at the ballpark, to facilitate my introductions and re-introductions to those family members, friends, and colleagues who have gone before me. I firmly believe that reunion with relatives and friends is often an ignored social part of eternal life that Christians and others hold as part of their faiths. In addition, I also look forward to joining that lively Irish chorus of spirit-singers who make music and song now and again on MacGillycuddy's Reeks in County Kerry, on other high peaks, and in cemeteries around the world to bolster hope and humor for those family members and friends who still remain on earth.